CONCOURS D'ELEGANCE

CONCOURS D'ELEGANCE

Dream cars and lovely ladies

PATRICK LESUEUR

Translated by David Burgess-Wise

DALTON WATSON FINE BOOKS

© E-T-A-I, 2011
First published in French-language by E-T-A-I in June 2011,
under the title *Concours d'élégance, le rêve automobile*
ISBN 978-2-7268-9542-9

E-T-A-I, Antony Parc 2,
10 place du général de Gaulle,
92160 ANTONY – France

US edition in English published in 2011
by Dalton Watson Fine Books
ISBN 978-1-85443-250-6

Printed in China by Toppan Leefung
for the publisher

Dalton Watson Fine Books
Deerfield, IL 60015
USA

www.daltonwatson.com

Contents

INTRODUCTION

The classic concept of the concours d'élégance may seem outmoded in an age when the most banal situations can be instantly captured on camera by a mobile phone, but nevertheless from the 1920s to the mid-1960s, these events were a vibrant window on the world of high fashion, luxury and creativity with – let's face it – a dash of sex-appeal. Each year the high season was the opportunity for towns like Paris, Hyères, Cannes, Deauville, Le Touquet, Biarritz, La Baule, Bordeaux and Vichy to form the backdrop for a marriage between the most daring creations of the coachbuilders with the latest designs from the fertile imaginations of the great Parisian couturiers.

The finishing touch was that indispensable ingredient of such occasions: the ladies. These visions of loveliness invariably had a dog in their train, whether it be a Scottie dog, an Afghan hound or a wire-haired terrier, to enhance their image. Fashionable spas and seaside resorts alike quickly realised that having a concours d'élégance for automobiles was an important ingredient of their summer schedule.

These events evolved year by year, with contestants increasingly choosing outfits that harmonised with the colours of the coachwork. The audience enthusiastically applauded ladies who changed their dress and hat according to their car. That was a touch of class that even the strictest jury in the world could hardly resist.

The task of this jury was to decide between the contestants, to place them in order and award the prizes, and its members were an elite selection from the world of high fashion. Broadly, these 'beauty contests' organised by magazines such as *L'Intransigeant*, *L'Auto* and the monthly *Fémina* brought together couturiers like Joseph Paquin, Lanvin, Madeleine Vionnet, Lucien Lelong, Maggy Rouff, Schiaparelli, Poiret, Worth and Jacques Fath (though the iconoclastic Coco Chanel wrote 'I don't like concours d'élégance … they seem grotesque to me…') with top carrossiers like Chapron, Binder, Franay, Kellner, Labourdette, Saoutchik, Figoni, Letourneur & Marchand, Million-Guiet, Pourtout and many others.

The 'Chauffeuses' were recruited from the whole spectrum of Parisian society – singers, actresses and variety artistes from the world of show business, but also society ladies from the noble houses of France and elsewhere. And there were one-time working girls whose charms had elevated them to the nobility, like Suzanne Berthier who, through a fortunate encounter, was henceforth known as Madame la Comtesse du Val de la Guillaumière, or Stella Mudge, former exotic dancer at the Folies Bergère and daughter of a high-wire walking Cockney pub landlord, who became the third wife of the Maharajah Paramjit Singh of the Indian princely state of Kapurthala, and who had her wedding-present Talbot-Lago 'Goutte d'Eau' repainted and retrimmed to match her frocks at concours.

In its August 1933 edition, *Fémina* waxed lyrical in describing the concours d'élégance it had organised in the Bois de Boulogne: 'The sun, which had been sulking all week, deigned to join the party that morning, adding blond highlights to the beauty of the girls and striking extra reflections from the shiny paintwork of the cars. It was a delightful display of elegance, luxury and good taste. At 8 o'clock the ceremonies began with the Concours d'Élégance and Coachwork Technique organised by our fellow publication *L'Auto*, which enjoyed its usual success. At 10 o'clock, the jury assembled by *L'Intransigeant* and *Fémina* under the presidency of M. André de Fouquières was seated, like St Louis, beneath the foliage of an ancient tree, and the business of the day could commence.

'Small cars first, followed by larger cars, paraded one by one as their names were called. And as each contestant went by, M. André de Fouquières offered a polite or witty remark and, according to merit, flowers or banners. The cash awards would be given at the end of the concours, during the drinks reception at the Cascade. In fact, they could not be awarded until late in the afternoon as the awarding of points was made difficult by the near impossibility of making a fair choice between so many magnificent performances.'

ANDRÉ DE FOUQUIÈRES, THE IMPARTIAL JUDGE

Mention is made in that report of a figure inseparable from such events, André de Fouquières (1875–1959), who was at the same time man of the world, chronicler, playwright, reporter, traveller, and diplomat. Scion of an ancient family from the Artois region of France, he was the son of the essayist and historian Louis de Fouquières who wrote of the classical poets Chénier and Ronsard, the great nephew of the 19th century society painter Alfred de Dreux and the brother of Pierre de Fouquières, who was usher to ambassadors. As a lecturer, André de Fouquières crossed continents and was welcome in every royal court in Europe as a living symbol of French traditions; his writings offer tasty titbits that reflect the everyday life of a certain epoch. A liaison officer with the British and American armies during the Great War who had been decorated with the Légion d'Honneur, the Croix de Guerre and the Military Cross, he had also earned numerous

ANDRÉ DE FOUQUIÈRES

CINQUANTE ANS

DE

Panache

PIERRE HORAY
"FLORE"

No concours d'élégance would have been complete without the informed and witty commentary of André de Fouquières, embodiment of French tradition and, on that account, welcomed in all the courts of Europe. These events were, by his reckoning, the high point of grace and beauty allied to power.
(GILLES BLANCHET COLLECTION)

foreign decorations in his many missions, where he had always shown himself an effective and informed propagandist in his various areas of expertise. He was often mocked for his uncommonly elitist side and been satirised as a presenter of rosettes, the host of a beauty contest or even the master of ceremonies of a seaside flower festival!

Another discordant element, particularly after the rise of the left-wing Front Populaire coalition government in 1936, was that André de Fouquières hardly seemed a committed republican, certainly judged by the association that he had founded in his youth, the 'White Carnation', whose task was to form a guard of honour for the Duke of Orléans, pretender to the French throne, then in exile in Brussels.

However, his distinguished ancestry and aristocratic demeanour hadn't prevented André de Fouquières from being appreciated by a wider public at these concours d'élégance. They recognised his talents as a speaker and his fund of stories, for André had no equal in humorously picturing in well-chosen words a pretty contestant who had inadvertently stalled her straight-eight or the grumpy bulldog that, when on parade before the jury, refused to quit the comfy bench seat of his mistress's formal saloon!

THE END OF THE AFFAIR

In 1951, Éditions Pierre Horay published the memoirs of André de Fouquières under the unequivocal title of *Cinquante Ans de Panache* ('Fifty years of cutting a dash'). It contains some tasty morsels:

'The radiator mascot had been elevated to the status of jewellery,' he observed wryly. 'That was the year when reptile skins garnished the interior of the coachwork and the exterior of their fair drivers, when the slightest touch on a button delivered a cigarette to your lips already lit or a put a powder puff to your nose. And that's not forgetting the thousand refinements that made a saloon car resemble the boudoir of the goddess Persephone.'

Later on he observed: 'Naturally the dress and hat, plus the personal seductiveness of the contestant, were valuable factors, as was the impeccable chauffeur – a coloured chauffeur for preference – for those who had not yet secured their diploma from the University of Versigny.' The latter establishment was a celebrated Parisian driving school of the day.

With a hint of irony, the man of the world continued: 'Here's a blonde in an almond green outfit, here's a brunette in a grey frock with silver stripes; one is discreet, the other provocative, one smiles at her lover, the other is anxiously anticipating a fine adventure. Here are the auburn locks and huge eyes of (the actress and singer) Renée Weiler who became the wife of (the playwright) Steve Passeur, and those big eyes and hair-do peeping out from under a hat would be recognised by the public at dress-rehearsals.'

In his work, André de Fouquières insisted that the great advantage of these concours was that everyone went home more or less satisfied. In effect, the jury handed out an impressive quantity of banners of honour, for excellence, for first class, of exceptional merit, and so forth. In short, every entrant could therefore be rewarded for… the line of the machines or the imagination behind the ensemble; their lightness, audacity, classicism, wisdom, and even craziness – they all figured in the prize list. And the prizes were awarded in categories.

They were sorted into cars created by the great coachbuilders, a category subdivided into open cars, closed cars (whether inside drive, coupés, two and four-door limousines…). As for so-called convertible cars, you found models with open fronts and opening roofs, as well as cabriolets with two or four side windows.

Coming then to cars whose bodywork came from the workshops of the manufacturers, in those cases the categories for open, closed and convertible cars were

the same. Then, in the mid-1930s, the 'streamline' trend from the United States sprang up
with renewed vigour, and suddenly the lines of many national models were transformed,
adopting raked windscreens, inclined radiators, enveloping wings and long tapering tails,
while a further category was created for aerodynamic coachwork to encompass cars like
the wildly streamlined Renault Grand Sport, the 'beaver-tailed' Peugeots and cars like the
Voisin Aérodyne.

Undeniably, the interwar years remain the high point of prestige and ostentation in
this domain. The irreplaceable André de Fouquières made a final allusion in the
framework of a more recent epoch: 'On a star-studded night in 1950, the automobile
concours d'élégance experienced a veritable renaissance on the Place Vendôme, which
was celebrating its bicentenary. In this admirable setting, which had been clothed once
more in ostentatious finery, under the spotlights and the dazzling glare of multicoloured
lamps, manufacturers and coachbuilders had entrusted their masterpieces to the most
exquisite actresses and the prettiest girls from the world of high fashion. That night, you
felt that Paris really had regained its former prestige.'

But the times had definitely changed. The difficult years of industrial reconstruction

in France drew a brutal halt to these events, from then on regarded as sheer frivolity. Besides, when you ordered a plebeian Renault 4CV in 1950, you often had to wait a year after putting down a deposit of 10,000 francs. You also had to pay a further 70,000 francs six months before taking delivery, so it was only after a full year that you at last got behind the wheel.

In addition, the prestigious reputation of French coachbuilders was coasting on its prewar renown, sticking to a traditional method of working that involved clothing overweight, obsolete chassis in raiment that was often ungainly and overloaded in an attempt to appear modern.

Flashes of brilliance were still possible, but we have to realise that today this admiration rests more on a nostalgic backwards glance than a true assessment in relation to the trends of the day.

From the early 1950s, an aristocracy would fade away and the concept of the pontoon wing, perfectly integrated into the rest of the bodywork, would prepare to rule the roost. The dominant trend came principally from the transatlantic constructors, who had been first to integrate design studios into their operations, a method of working rapidly adopted by manufacturers worldwide.

Nevertheless, concours d'élégance clung on into the 1960s, like the famous display on the shores of the Lac d'Enghien in the Ile de France. While the show business stars were still on hand, the cars with one-off bodywork were mostly replaced by production models that could only be told from the versions seen in the showrooms of dealers and importers by their non-standard paintwork and accessories.

Ford-France's V8 Vedette – originally intended as a 'compact' model for the USA market – was the undoubted star of the October 1948 Paris Salon. From then on, this subsidiary of the American giant was a regular entrant in many concours d'élégance. This photo clearly shows how things were organised, with the friendly commentator on the left and the young girl and her escort in the middle. Beyond the car is the crowd, at once attentive, admiring and impressed. The car, on 'WO' trade plates, has its entry number in the windscreen.
(© GILLES BLANCHET COLLECTION)

It's difficult to tell from this photo which classes these charming young competitors have won. The one on the right certainly has a cup whose size suggests she's won a 'Grand Prix d'Excellence'. It's noteworthy that in those happy days no classy lady would venture forth in public without wearing a hat by a famous milliner.

(© GILLES BLANCHET COLLECTION)

FROM THE ROARING TWENTIES TO WORLD WAR TWO

AFTER THE DREADFUL HUMAN TRAGEDY OF THE FIRST WORLD WAR, THE FRENCH AND THEIR EUROPEAN NEIGHBOURS HOPED ONCE MORE TO FIND TRUE HAPPINESS AND WILLINGLY LET THEMSELVES BE CARRIED ALONG BY THE SHEER JOY OF LIVING. THE PROGRESSIVE DEMOCRATISATION OF THE MOTOR CAR MARKED AN IMPORTANT STEP IN THE QUEST FOR A NEW SENSE OF WELL-BEING: IT WAS NOW POSSIBLE FOR MANY PEOPLE TO BUY A CAR! THE CREATIVITY OF THE MOTORING MOVEMENT ALSO GENERATED SUMPTUOUS SPECTACLES THAT MIRRORED EVERY POSSIBLE LUXURY, WHERE THE MOST EXUBERANT AND INNOVATIVE MODELS WERE DISPLAYED. THESE SHOWY SPECTACLES WERE KNOWN AS CONCOURS D'ELEGANCE AND REACHED THEIR PEAK IN THE INTERWAR YEARS, UNDENIABLY THE RICHEST PERIOD IN THIS FIELD.

You didn't need to be high-born to compete in an elitist contest among the most elegant of all!
The proof is this 1924 model 6CV Renault Type KJ1. With a modest 950cc engine, this little beauty
carries all-weather tourer bodywork by Muhlbacher. (© PHOTOTHÈQUE RENAULT COMMUNICATION/DR)

In 1923, the young Citroën company launched an updated version of the 10-hp Type B2 range which could be told from the previous season's model by the 16 louvres in its bonnet. The three-seat fixed-head coupé with its oval side windows wasn't lacking in personality, proving once more that high-priced chassis didn't have a monopoly on style.
(© PHOTOTHÈQUE CITROËN COMMUNICATION/DR)

Even though this advertisement for the 1924 Peugeot 10 CV Luxe Type 177 B – also available in boat-tailed 'Sport' guise – wasn't specifically issued in connection with a concours d'élégance, it perfectly encapsulates the elitist spirit of these events that married beautiful coachwork with the world of fashion. It was by the talented designer René Vincent, whose work illustrated the catalogues of many high-class marques. (PATRICK LESUEUR COLLECTION)

Concours d'élégance also offered a marvellous backdrop against which art coachbuilders could unveil their most iconoclastic creations, like this design on a Panhard chassis by Jean-Henri Labourdette, shown on 3 June 1926 in the Parc des Princes. Distinguishing features include the sponson steps and the wind-cheating wing profiles. (© GILLES BLANCHET COLLECTION)

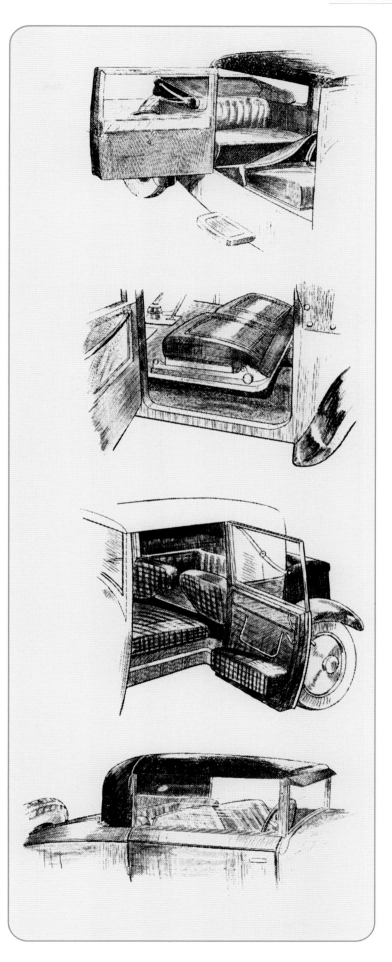

These sketches that appeared in *Moto Revue* give some idea of the different possible arrangements for two-door bodywork. From top to bottom: a Bugatti cabriolet, a Chenard & Walker, another Bugatti cabriolet and finally a Manessius close-coupled drophead with room for four inside plus another two in the dickey seat.

(© GILLES BLANCHET COLLECTION)

Taken in 1933, this photograph reveals a coming trend.
The open drive town car would become an automotive
status symbol emblematic of the discriminating rich,
who could nonchalantly ignore the financial troubles of
consumers at large. The elegant lady beside this
Binder-bodied Renault Reinasport is the operatic
soprano Marthe Chenal, still dubbed 'the most
beautiful woman in Paris' at the age of 52. The sheer
class of the *tout ensemble* with its attentive chauffeurs
earned it First Grand Prix d'Honneur at *L'Auto*'s
concours in the Bois de Boulogne.

(© GILLES BLANCHET COLLECTION)

Here's a real puzzle picture! Taken at an unknown location –possibly some local festival in the south of France – it raises the question as to whether any top-notch concours would admit such a casually-dressed team. Were they, perhaps, the local lifeguards at a fashionable resort? The car – a natty Peugeot 5 CV Type 172-R Grand Sport, introduced in 1926 for the typically Twenties 'Smart Young Things' market – is certainly stylish enough, and its pointed tail proudly declares, 'Peugeot – la marque nationale'. (© GILLES BLANCHET COLLECTION)

This Chenard & Walcker built in Gennevilliers around 1927 carries a sober saloon body by coachbuilder Million-Guiet, founded as long ago as 1854. Based in Levallois, Million-Guiet made a great leap forward a short while after this picture was taken by adopting the frameless 'Toutalu' sheet metal construction patented by the aviator Jean de Vizcaya.

(© GILLES BLANCHET COLLECTION)

The 1926 Paris Salon saw the unveiling of the new Citroën B14, powered by a four-in-line sidevalve engine of 1538cc, developing an actual 22 hp. Citroën's interior drive models had an undeniably classic style, even if it was beauty on a budget. Only the drophead coupés added a lighter touch to the company catalogue. (© PHOTOTHÈQUE CITROËN COMMUNICATION/DR)

The cheerily smiling young lady in the coat with elegantly scalloped edges is leaning against a six-cylinder 18 CV Talbot (Darracq in England) Type TL Sport with fabric-covered Weymann flexible coachwork. (PATRICK LESUEUR COLLECTION)

The actress Maud Loty participated in the concours d'élégance of the Automobile Club de Nice with this Fiat saloon, registered in the Alpes-Maritimes region in October 1928. The polished aluminium wheel discs and tubular bumpers give the vehicle a very trendy look. If popular gossip was to be believed, Miss Loty's greyhound 'Mitsou' was insured for the tidy sum of a million francs.

(© GILLES BLANCHET COLLECTION)

Just as famous couturiers set the trend when they show their collections, so the renowned coachbuilders unveiled their creations as the great concours d'élégance drew near. The magnificent profile of this 1928 design by the Belgian coachbuilder Willy Van Den Plas, who ran an outpost of the paternal Brussels-based company in Paris between 1924–34, proves that a simple white belt-line was a sure sign of speed, even when the car was stationary. (© GILLES BLANCHET COLLECTION)

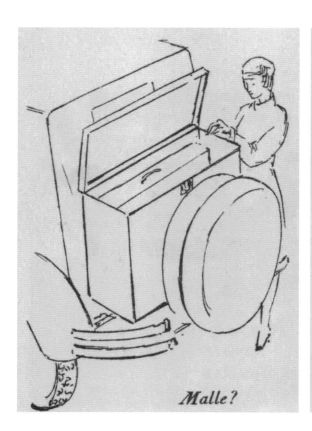

Malle?

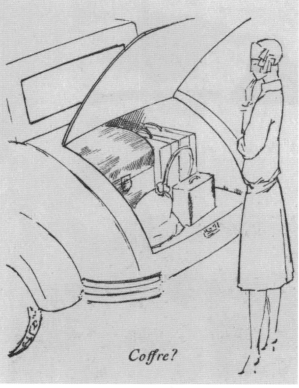

Coffre?

At the end of the 1920s, opinion was divided between those who preferred detachable trunks and those who liked integral boots. The drawback of the built-in boot was that it restricted passenger space, but it was easier to pack. While a trunk wasn't an integral part of the vehicle, it collected dust and made washing the car more difficult as it was hard to get underneath. Finally, the boot won the day by giving a neat finish to the lines of a saloon or tourer.

(© GILLES BLANCHET COLLECTION)

Italy's automobile industry possessed a make capable of rivalling the most prestigious marques of Europe and America in the Fabbrica Automobili Isotta-Fraschini, located in the via Monterosa in Milan. This short-chassis Tipo 8A or 8A SS, powered by a 5902cc straight-eight with two overhead valves per cylinder and developing 135-150 hp, won top honours at the concours d'élégance organised by the spa town of Vichy. (© MUSÉE DE L'OPÉRA DE VICHY)

The Citroën AC 4 went on the market at the beginning of 1929. This six-window saloon is all ready for a fashionable clientele: two-tone paint, aluminium wheel discs, two-blade bumpers. With its low, well-balanced profile this car no longer has the starchy style characteristic of the marque's earliest closed bodyshells.

(© PHOTOTHÈQUE CITROËN COMMUNICATION/DR)

This 1928 32 CV Hispano-Suiza has benefited from the skilled attentions of the panel beaters of the old-established coachbuilders Belvalette, based at 21 de la rue Duret in Paris. Its Duco cellulose finish offered a rich palette of colours and had the great advantage of not fading after a few months. (© GILLES BLANCHET COLLECTION)

The Citroën B14 G wasn't listed in such a luxurious guise in the catalogue of the Quai de Javel firm. This example was ordered by a wealthy client who wanted matt silver leather upholstery, which he claimed was more restful! (© GILLES BLANCHET COLLECTION)

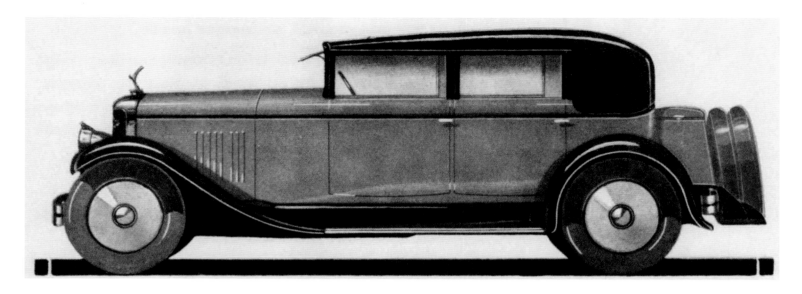

For his part, the coachbuilder Maurice Proux of Courbevoie envisioned this comfortable saloon with a more conservative, yet undeniably handsome, profile enhanced by twin spare wheels mounted behind the external trunk. Once again, a judiciously-placed belt-line played an important part in the composition. (© GILLES BLANCHET COLLECTION)

When in Paris, HRH Princesse Mediba Djelal of Egypt chose to take the air in this sporty but nevertheless exceedingly comfortable cabriolet built on a six cylinder Talbot (Darracq) chassis, another example of custom coachwork by Maurice Proux. (© GILLES BLANCHET COLLECTION)

European sales of 'America's Mightiest Motor Car', the 265 hp twin-cam straight-eight Model J Duesenberg, were handled by Edmond Z. Sadovich's Motors de Luxe of 12 Rue de Berri, Paris, who commissioned Europe's finest coachbuilders to body the imported chassis. Duesenbergs – sold as 'the most expensive car in the world' – won many concours prizes in France, including this elegant convertible cabriolet which carried off the Grand Prix d'Honneur at the Vichy concours d'élégance.
(© MUSÉE DE L'OPÉRA DE VICHY)

As the winter of 1928 drew near, the immodestly self-styled *'carrossier d'art'* (artistic coachbuilder) Felber, whose showrooms were at 71 Avenue des Champs-Élysées, conceived this all-weather saloon, registered design 22384. Its long bonnet was combined with a roofline made as low as possible in the quest for a perfectly balanced silhouette. (© GILLES BLANCHET COLLECTION)

The new monthly magazine *La Mode Automobile* was launched in October 1928 by André Girard. In its pages, the magazine reported on nearly every concours d'élégance held in France. The cover design – rather daring for the period – neatly combined the two icons of such events, feminine charm and the elegant lines of an automobile.

Panhard's most discriminating clients ordered the 35 CV Type X54 chassis, which had an impressive sleeve-valve straight-eight engine displacing 6.35 litres. This coupé de ville has bodywork by Janssen & Cie of Levallois-Perret, a quality coachbuilder founded by Claude Janssen in 1902 that specialised in bodying Panhards in the interwar years. By the end of the 1920s, wood-spoked wheels were looking a trifle passé. (© GILLES BLANCHET COLLECTION)

The iconoclastic coachbuilder Guillaume Busson of Nanterre (Seine) created this avant-garde 'torpedo roadster' body on what looks like an Amilcar chassis in the late 1920s. Its skirted wings, lack of running boards and fastback boot were features well ahead of their time. Sadly, Busson was declared bankrupt in 1933 and went to work for Gaston Grummer.

(© GILLES BLANCHET COLLECTION)

This stylish composition by William Aguet appeared in the automobile press in the autumn of 1928, advertising the coachbuilder Maurice Proux of Courbevie (Seine). Proux entered 17 cars in the concours organised by *L'Auto* in 1929, and 15 reached the final. A remarkable coupé de ville by Proux on an rare Cord L29 chassis with a daring pearl grey finish shown on the Auburn-Cord stand at the Paris Salon of 1930 sold on the spot.

(© GILLES BLANCHET COLLECTION)

Opposite page: True to its name, *La Mode Automobile* inspired its female readers with ideas for motoring outfits. The dress is decorated with ornaments influenced by the world of the car: a bracelet like a stone-guard, buttons like hubcaps, a brooch like bumpers. But lady, beware! Such accessories were not available off the shelf but needed to be created.

(© GILLES BLANCHET COLLECTION)

Whether car or high fashion, fine lines enhanced the form. It was a simple effect, shown to great advantage in the drawing where the plain dress of the lady is given added interest by coloured stripes, echoed in the pinstripes on the car body.

(© GILLES BLANCHET COLLECTION)

Above: at Nice in the summer of 1930, Prince Farid's Type RM Reinastella convertible town car was paraded before the jury by Mlle d'Orgères. The chauffeur and his assistant are decked out in full dress: white overcoats with black velvet collars. This elegant machine is bodied by the aristocratic coachbuilder Kellner, inventors of the 'scaphandrier' (deep-sea diver) tourer which had a convertible rear compartment.
(© PHOTOTHÈQUE RENAULT COMMUNICATION/SADI PHOTO)

Wide-brimmed felt hats, or quilted velvet numbers, decorated with the feathers of cockerels or egrets, the plumage of ostrich or birds of paradise... it was impossible to take part in a concours without a hat from some well-known milliner. Most fashionable were Reboux, Jane Blanchot, Germaine Page and Maria Guy. (© GILLES BLANCHET COLLECTION)

Magdeleine, Comtesse de Ganay, one of the three daughters of the industrialist and financier Edouard Gouïn who all married well, smiles proudly from the comfortable cockpit of her 41 CV 7125cc straight-eight Renault Type RM 1 Reinastella with factory custom cabriolet coachwork which has the uncommon option of wire wheels. She had just won the 1930 Paris-Cannes Rallye Féminin with this stylish car, capable of a top speed of 85 mph. She would also win the following year's Paris-Amsterdam Rallye Féminin in this car. (© GILLES BLANCHET COLLECTION)

At the 1928 Paris Salon, André Citroën followed the fashion for six-cylinder cars and launched the AC6, with a 45 hp 2.5-litre engine. Available from the spring of 1929, this generously-proportioned Grand Tourisme C6 E saloon was fitted with a capacious steel trunk. The radiator script leaves the fitment of the new power unit in no doubt. And no young lady of fashion would be seen in public without a cloche hat. (© PHOTOTHÈQUE CITROËN COMMUNICATION/DR)

Accompanied by a charming young hostess, this Citroën C6 F two-seater coupé is competing in the 1931 concours d'élégance on the greensward of the Parc des Princes. The jazz-painted doors recall the work of modernist painters like Fernand Léger or Robert Delaunay. Notable are the central step, the cycle-type wings, the radiator stoneguard and the bolt-on wire wheels. (© GILLES BLANCHET COLLECTION)

The main entrance of the *très chic* Tennis Country Club at La Baule, where three smart dropheads are taking part in the September 1930 concours d'élégance. The body of the first car, a short-wheelbase Delage D8, is almost certainly by Saoutchik, while the second in line is an L-29 Cord, a car rarely seen on European roads. The third car looks like a Delage, too. (© GILLES BLANCHET COLLECTION)

CONCOURS D'ELEGANCE DE BAGATELLE, JUNE 1932; BILLANCOURT TAKES ON THE WORLD

France was one of the last countries to be affected by the world-wide depression, but the country was in crisis by 1932. Nevertheless, the magazine *L'Officiel de la Mode* declared that, 'at first sight, you might doubt that the June season in Paris has been affected and tarnished by the pitiless crisis that is sweeping over us.' That year, Renault offered a range that went from the humble Monaquatre Type UY, with a basic price of 18,400 francs, to the six-cylinder Monastella, Primastella and Vivastella, costing at least from 26,500 to 52, 000 francs. On top of that, after the famous 9140cc straight-six 40 CV Type NM was discontinued in 1928, the flagship of the range became the 7125cc Type RM Reinastella, Renault's first straight-eight, homologated in September 1928.

In 1932 Renault listed two straight-eight ranges, the 4.2 litre Nervastella (types TG2 and TG3) and Nervasport (type TG5) and the long-bonneted Reinastella, which was the Renault for an elite class, with chassis prices ranging from 150,000 to 170,000 francs. These were the Renault models that achieved top honours in the various concours d'élégance, either with factory bodywork or coachwork by the most fashionable carrossiers.

If Louis Renault was courageous in continuing to build such outstanding machines to uphold the reputation of his eponymous marque in the face of fierce competition from home and overseas, his production figures continued to hold steady. And even today a mass-production manufacturer can find it difficult to successfully market that kind of top-of-the-range model alongside his more modest offerings.

This young lady seems lost in the vast expanse of sheet metal that makes up this dual-cowl Reinastella tourer, the work of the coachbuilder Dubos of Neuilly-sur-Seine. If this maker was not lacking in ingenuity, he was still a minor figure compared with the top French coachbuilders. The immense length of this car is further exaggerated by the absence of side-mounted spares; the wheels have been relegated to the rear of the car to preserve an unbroken silhouette.
(© PHOTOTHÈQUE RENAULT COMMUNICATION/DR)

Million-Guiet also created this impressive dual-cowl Reinastella tourer with its twin vee-screens, top award winner at the 1932 Bagatelle Concours d'Élégance, though on this type of open coachwork the hallmarks of that coachbuilder are less apparent. The curved profile of the tail is an unusual feature. (© PHOTOTHÈQUE RENAULT COMMUNICATION/DR)

Even more original were the creations of the house of Million-Guiet, founded in 1854 as carriage makers. In January 1930 Million-Guiet purchased the 'Toutalu' patent applied for two years earlier by the young aviator Jean de Vizcaya for a system of frameless body construction using light-alloy panels fastened together to form a rigid structure. A distinctive feature of these Million-Guiet bodies was the rounded edges of the windows. The toolbox on the running board has an aesthetic all its own. (© PHOTOTHÈQUE RENAULT COMMUNICATION/DR)

'To buy French is a national duty,' declared Renault in March 1932, the same month that the company introduced the 24 CV Nervasport TG5, a brand new sporting model extrapolated from the Nervastella, with a 10 ft 3 in wheelbase instead of 12 ft 4 in. Its 4250cc straight-eight engine gave a top speed, outstanding for the period, of almost 90 mph.

(© PHOTOTHÈQUE RENAULT COMMUNICATION/DR)

In 1932 the Renault Reinastella adopted a handsome new radiator shell greatly inspired by that of the Chrysler Imperial launched the previous year. New, too, were the five opening vents in each side of the bonnet. This 'torpedo scaphandrier' is typical of Kellner, whose boss Jacques Kellner was a hero of the French Resistance, executed by the Gestapo in Paris' Mont Valérien prison in March 1942.
(© PHOTOTHÈQUE RENAULT COMMUNICATION/DR)

More modest than its eight-cylinder big sisters presented on that occasion, but nevertheless very elegant, this Primastella Type PG6 powered by a 4050cc six-cylinder engine also took part in the event. It appears to be a works sports roadster with a folding windscreen. That year a new PG8 Primastella saloon with opening vents on the bonnet sides was added to the range.
(© PHOTOTHÈQUE RENAULT COMMUNICATION/DR)

This bizarre town car with a rear like a Hansom cab appears to have been commissioned by a rich fresh-air fiend if it wasn't just for use in the summer! Distinctive features are the sham canework on the sides of the passenger compartment and the coach lamps emphasising the horse-drawn carriage aspect of the design. Noteworthy, too, are the anachronistic spoked wheels and the folding windscreen.
(© PHOTOTHÈQUE RENAULT COMMUNICATION/DR)

The London coachbuilder Freestone & Webb displays a remarkable fluidity of line with this two-door saloon on a Delage D8 chassis, powered by a pushrod straight-eight engine of 4 litres capacity. The triangular vents in the bonnet sides are an unusual touch. Founded in 1920, Freestone & Webb were more usually associated with Bentley, Rolls-Royce and Mercedes-Benz chassis and were not afraid to innovate. (© GILLES BLANCHET COLLECTION)

Spectators at the La Baule concours in the summer of 1931 are as appreciative of the attractive lines of the crew as of the elegant form of this Bugatti Type 51 cabriolet with its 3.3-litre straight-eight engine. Decidedly trendy at the time is its 'Flèche d'Argent' (Silver Arrow) front bumper made by the Cromos accessory company of Levallois.

(© GILLES BLANCHET COLLECTION)

This Renault Nervasport is the work of Henri Chapron of Levallois-Perret, possibly France's most prolific coachbuilder. Enhanced by the irresistible charms of film actress Simone Jarnac, star of *Le Bébé de l'Escadron* (*Baby of the Squadron*), this cabriolet stands out for its bold two-tone paint finish and its chromed wire wheels. The formally-garbed chauffeur, more suitably dressed for a staid town car, seems to be waiting in the wings for his turn. Founded in Neuilly-sur-Seine in 1920, Chapron remained in business until 1985.
(© PHOTOTHÈQUE RENAULT COMMUNICATION/DR)

A less appropriate backdrop for this delightful Amilcar roadster ('Don't dump garbage', reads the sign) could scarcely have been chosen. Probably built on a modest 1929 vintage 7 CV Amilcar CGSS sports chassis with a four-cylinder 1100cc engine, the little car has an extended bonnet hinting at the installation of the Saint-Denis firm's potent twin-cam straight six from the C6 competition model. Sadly, the name of the constructor of the polished metal bodywork has been lost, but the cycle wings and the jaunty wheel discs, as well as the lack of running boards, are all indicative of the devil-may-care attitude of sporting motorists in the Roaring Twenties.

(PATRICK LESUEUR COLLECTION)

Despite its status as a mass-producer, Citroën added three C6G Spéciales to its standard catalogue for 1932. The firm was aiming them at a clientele that was seeking both originality and refinement. The bodies of these latest additions were entrusted to outside coachbuilders. The astounding 'Toutalu' close-coupled saloon was built in the shops of Million-Guiet, while the all-weather saloon and its closed version were the work of the Société Industrielle de Carrosserie Automobile in Levallois. Needless to say, these three models were proud defenders of the honour of Citroën in the most popular concours d'élégance.

(© PHOTOTHÈQUE CITROËN COMMUNICATION/DR)

While the Renault Reinastella still had right-hand drive in 1932, the short wheelbase sporting version, the Reinasport RM-5, adopted left-hand drive. This magnificent drophead photographed in Bordeaux enjoys a judiciously balanced colour scheme in contrasting tones, along with hand painted whitewall Michelin 15×46 tyres. The little plaque above the running board indicates 'Stella', the sign of great distinction at Billancourt.

(© GILLES BLANCHET COLLECTION)

This photograph from 1933 encapsulates the magnificence of the concours d'élégance where creativity was ranked under three different headings: fashion, coachwork and automotive technology. This winning combination shows the lovely film star Nadine Picard with the 4-litre 23 CV Delage D8-Sport 'YoYo' pillarless coupe by Letourneur & Marchand. The Yoyo or Diabolo style, part of an extraordinary artistic movement, featured such gimmicks as the circular bonnet vents, the audacious shape of the greenhouse and the continuous sweep of the side windows. (© GILLES BLANCHET COLLECTION)

There's no indication on this photo that this sumptuous 1932 Bugatti Type 50-T coupé is on its way to a concours d'élégance, but its perfectly harmonious lines, due to the customary inspiration of Jean Bugatti, would certainly earn it a Grand Prix d'Honneur. Noteworthy are the capacious trunk, the twin spare wheels at the rear and the assiduous juxtaposition of the two-tone colour scheme. Under the bonnet is a twin-cam straight-eight of 4970cc, force-fed by a supercharger to develop some 200 hp, giving a top speed of around 120 mph, an outstanding performance for 1932.

(PATRICK LESUEUR COLLECTION)

week-end en rivière

Votre
301
à Roues Avant
Indépendantes
première au ponton
...Votre
bateau
fin prêt pour la
régate

Peugeot

This striking advertisement from 1933 places an 8 CV Peugeot 8 CV Type 301 in the leisurely, but rather chic, setting of a regatta, a milieu not far removed from that of the concours d'élégance. The Peugeot 301, launched in the summer of 1932, was promoted as a development of the 201. The wheelbase of its rigid 'Bloctube' chassis was longer than that of the 201, enabling the construction of six-light saloons. (© GILLES BLANCHET COLLECTION)

One can see the influence of the leading American coachwork designers in this 1933 vintage Renault Nervasport cabriolet, which looks impressively powerful against the frail form of Mlle Mougeot. She presented it at the Nice concours to such good effect that the combination carried off the first prize for elegance. Its long bonnet and compact passenger compartment are a sure-fire recipe for creating a perfect rolling sculpture. (© PHOTOTHÈQUE RENAULT COMMUNICATION/DR)

There was little daring about the bodies produced by the famed coachbuilder Henri Binder of the Rue du Colisée in Paris, but they were distinguished by their good taste and classic elegance. Ample evidence is given by this coupé de ville based on a Renault Reinastella chassis which was shown at the summer 1933 concours d'élégance in Nice.
(© PHOTOTHÈQUE RENAULT COMMUNICATION/DR)

This dainty duo makes a charming picture. Perhaps the horizontal and vertical lines on their dresses are intended to echo the radiator grilles of the cars on display. (© GILLES BLANCHET COLLECTION)

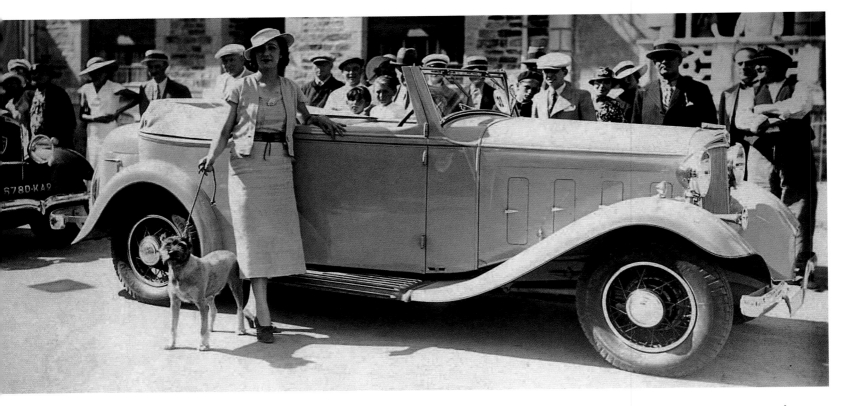

The 1933 models from the Suresnes Talbot factory had elegant wind-cheating radiators, a style recently arrived from the other side of the Atlantic that would point the way ahead in Europe. Beneath the bonnets of the Fulgur range beat potent modern in-line sixes available in taxable ratings of 11, 14 and 16 CV. Despite its exaggeratedly large rear end, doubtless linked to the high belt line, this cabriolet is not lacking in charm.

A huge crowd has been attracted to the 1933 edition of the concours d'élégance at the resort of Arcachon, and the visitors can certainly dream at leisure in the presence of the most prestigious automobiles, but also in front of more commonplace vehicles specially prepared for the occasion. It shouldn't be forgotten that at this period most French families relied on bicycles or public transport for their daily journeys.

(© PHOTOTHÈQUE RENAULT COMMUNICATION/DR)

Opposite: Taken during the high season of 1933 for the magazine *Fémina* in the Bois de Boulogne, not far from the famous Pré-Catelan restaurant, this photograph reveals what were known as sports outfits. Why? Because henceforth an elegant lady would spend several hours of her day in an automobile. An outfit for motoring would therefore be not only a sporty yet practical dress that would be kept for touring, but also a town dress for the morning and afternoon.

(© GILLES BLANCHET COLLECTION)

CONCOURS D'ÉLÉGANCE FÉMININE EN AUTOMOBILE

In June 1933 Pierre Lafitte and Robert Ochs, the directors of the monthly *Fémina*, and their fashion editor Martine Régnier organised a 'Concours d'Elégance Féminine en Automobile' (Feminine elegance in a car) in the Bois de Boulogne. From 10 in the morning, the distinguished jury gathered around its president André de Fouquières, and more than 200 cars followed each other in the Allée de Sèvres at Neuilly and from Bagatelle up to the Carrefour de Longchamp. These photos of the contestants give some idea of the richness of the entry.

The Premier Grand Prix d'Honneur was awarded to the soprano Marthe Chenal, at the wheel of an impressive coupé de ville bodied by Binder on a Renault Nervastella TG-4 chassis. The coachbuilder had chosen the longest wheelbase option of 11 ft 9 in for his creation. The long, long bonnet housed a 4.2-litre sidevalve engine developing 100 hp. In this photo taken at Monte Carlo, where the car won first prize, the chauffeur and under-chauffeur are impeccably dressed as an integral part of the presentation.
(© PHOTOTHÈQUE RENAULT COMMUNICATION/DR)

The charming Agnes Arley of the Théâtre des Nouveautés was another beauty who brought honours for Renault at this concours, winning the Prix des Voitures Transformables with this Reinasport faux cabriolet with sunshine roof, bodied by Kellner. The silhouette of the car has the hallmark touches of this coachbuilder, founded in 1860 by harnessmaker Georges Kellner, for it is elegant yet with a hint of austerity. (© PHOTOTHÈQUE RENAULT COMMUNICATION/DR)

The singer Lucienne Boyer, best known for her signature song 'Parlez-moi d'amour', smiles sweetly from her Renault Reinasport whose fluid lines were drafted by the American stylist Howard 'Dutch' Darrin, who teamed up with South American banker J. Fernandez to build custom bodies in an ultra-modern factory in Boulogne-sur-Seine, where 200 workmen produced around three bodies a fortnight. Note the trendy Cromos bumpers and the big spotlight by the windscreen. (© PHOTOTHÈQUE RENAULT COMMUNICATION/DR)

Though the mass-produced bodywork of this Peugeot 301 saloon doesn't seem to have aroused much interest in the crowd, nevertheless the lovely Marcelle Chantal – a film star who married a rich American – was rewarded with a Prix d'Honneur. Maybe her springtime dress by Lucien Lelong and her broad-brimmed hat by Lemonnier influenced the jury! The 8 CV from Sochaux was prepared for its concours appearance with a becoming light colour scheme, whitewall tyres and the bumpers that would appear on the 1934 models. (© GILLES BLANCHET COLLECTION)

Dressed in a pale green frock by Lucien Lelong, the film starlet Suzet Maïs looks fresher, prettier and more blonde than ever in her Peugeot 301 fixed-head coupé. Apart from the whitewall tyres (and possibly the colour scheme), the car appears to be quite standard. The registration indicates that it was put on the roads of the Seine département in April 1933.

(© GILLES BLANCHET COLLECTION)

Renault's PG 8 Primastella range was launched at the 1932 Paris Salon to replace the Monastella, dropped at the end of the previous season as the Billancourt company's six-cylinder 'starter range' to replace the Monastella, dropped at the end of the previous season. Louis Renault must have been taken by the styling of the 1931 season Chrysler CG Imperial, as the radiator shells of the 1932–33 Renaults were a close copy. (© PHOTOTHÈQUE RENAULT COMMUNICATION/DR)

The Berliet marque was rarely seen at concours events. This 9 CV Type 944 coupé is driven by fashion designer Yvet Lemonnier. This is the Grand Luxe version, optionally available with independent front suspension. Noteworthy are the innovative contrasting tones of the bodywork and the vast rear trunk. (© GILLES BLANCHET COLLECTION)

There were three models in the so-called 'flat-radiator' Delahaye range: the 10 CV Type 122 and 12 CV Type 124 with four-cylinder ohv engines and the six-cylinder 16 CV Type 126. The charming Mme Catineau-Pitray is leaning against a Type 124 bodied by Currus, a Parisian company founded in 1900 by Nathan Lévy and his 16-year-old son Samuel. Currus – the name is Latin for 'coach' – built both private and commercial coachwork. (© GILLES BLANCHET COLLECTION)

Mary Glory, who made her debut in films in 1924 and died in 2009, two months short of her 104th birthday, smiles confidently beside a smart 6 CV Fiat Ballila marketed in France by SAFAF – the predecessor of Henri Théodore Pigozzi's Simca firm – to prove that a modest 995cc roadster with an 7 ft 4 in wheelbase could hold its own in such august company. This little Fiat retailed at just 15,950 francs, while in contrast just the bare chassis of a Renault Reinasport would set you back 55,000 francs. (© GILLES BLANCHET COLLECTION)

Dressed in beige by Lucille Paray, with a little brown hat by the milliner Agnès, film star Renée Devillers stands proudly beside a 'Berline de Voyage' on the Peugeot 302 Type Confort chassis. This elegant body, whose imposing presence seems to indicate that it was built by an outside company, was strictly a production model – only the whitewall tyres were extra – that could be bought from any Peugeot dealer.
(© GILLES BLANCHET COLLECTION)

Madame la Baronne de Pitray took the wheel of a six-cylinder Delahaye Type 126 with four-door limousine coachwork by Labourdette at the concours. While Labourdette had a tradition of producing more audacious coachwork, oddly enough the jury was unanimous in awarding this more conventional design a Prix d'Honneur.
(© GILLES BLANCHET COLLECTION)

With a wheelbase of just 7 ft 4 in, this
5 CV Amilcar C3, with Cabriolet
Luxe bodywork built in-house at the
firm's St-Denis factory, proves that a
small car has its place in a concours
d'elégance. The chromed bumpers
and iridescent paintwork are non-
standard features specially added for
the sake of appearance.
(© GILLES BLANCHET COLLECTION)

The Comtesse Faur de Pibrac brings her Peugeot 301
8 CV 'Confort' drophead coupé, No 212 in the
parade, to a halt in front of the jury. This recently
introduced 'Coupé Golf' body style on the new
'Bloctube' chassis was also available with a fixed head
as the 'Coach Golf'. The car has such optional
features as Grebel headlamps, Chromos bumpers,
twin horns and a specially-finished radiator shell.
(© GILLES BLANCHET COLLECTION)

Oddly enough, this four/five seat drophead cabriolet, with which Mme Morin won the Grand Prix des Voitures Ouvertes, is an advance model of the 1934 Reinasport RM6, which was launched at the October 1933 Paris Salon. This was a sportier version of the 7125cc straight-eight Reinastella with an impressive top speed of almost 95 mph, but was only on the market a few months before it was replaced by the equally short-lived Reinasport ZS 1.

(© PHOTOTHÈQUE RENAULT COMMUNICATION/DR)

This young couple is posed alongside a Studebaker Dictator Six at Vichy in the summer of 1934. The little girl is finding it difficult to lean elegantly against the enclosed spare wheel, an optional fitting on this cabriolet, because of its height. Parked behind is an impressive Cadillac cabriolet, a product of the only company offering a range of V8, V12 and V16 automobiles at the time.

(© MUSÉE DE L'OPÉRA DE VICHY)

This Fiat registered in the Seine département in July 1934 is a saloon from SAFAF's new 11 CV catalogue. It was entered in a number of concours during the summer of that year by the company's founder and boss Henri Théodore Pigozzi, who would transform the company into Simca in November 1934, taking over the old Donnet works in Nanterre. A French version of the Tipo 518 Ardita, it has poetically-named *queues de comète* (comet's tail) mouldings concealing the cooling vents on the side of the bonnet.

(© MUSÉE DE L'OPÉRA DE VICHY)

With his unerring sense of publicity, André Citroën revealed his latest and most revolutionary creation, the Traction Avant, to the general public. In July 1934, Citroën's daughter Jacqueline is on parade beside a magnificent 7B or 7 Sport roadster, differing from standard in its single tone paint job and coach-lined wheel discs with chromed rims.

(© GILLES BLANCHET COLLECTION)

It would be impossible to show the Traction Avant roadster without also mentioning the highly appealing coupé (or faux cabriolet, as they referred to it at the time). It carries the trade registration plate of a dealership in Clermont-Ferrand. The front-wheel drive '7' was unveiled in style on 18 April 1934, at a time when the Citroën company was fighting for its life. Sadly André Citroën, who had invested body and soul in this innovative industrial project, would not live to see its happy ending, for he died prematurely on 3 July the following year, aged just 57.
In the lower picture, the same woman in a polka dot dress poses alongside her Traction Avant faux cabriolet at a Vichy concours. Note the decorative chrome spear on the door and the hand-painted whitewalls on the tyres. In 1935, this style of coachwork was available on the 7B, 7C, 11 Légère, 11 Normale and even on the mysterious 22 CV V8 shown at the 1934 Salon, which never passed the prototype stage. (© MUSÉE DE L'OPÉRA DE VICHY)

Seen in the summer of 1934, the brand-new (though rather middle-class) French-assembled Fiat Ardita would be built under the Simca banner at Nanterre alongside the 6 CV Ballila from mid-1935. Its promoter, one-time Piedmontese scrap merchant Henri Théodore Pigozzi, entered the model in several concours d'élégance during 1934. The odd flashes on the wings are rather kitsch, but the overall appearance is ordinary. (© GILLES BLANCHET COLLECTION)

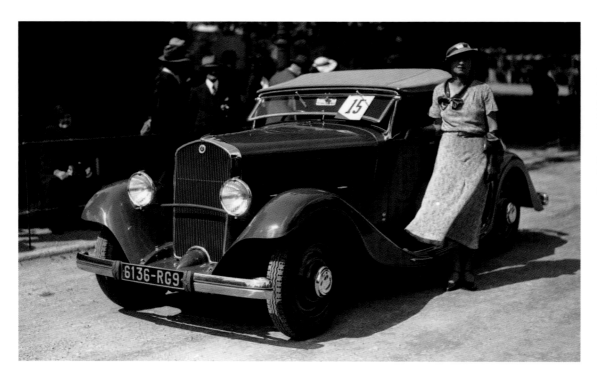

A stylish La Licorne 8 CV type L-764 cabriolet, with a retail price of 26,000 francs, first registered in January 1934 in the Seine département. Its 1450cc engine develops 24 hp at 3500 rpm, giving a modest top speed of some 55 mph.

(© GILLES BLANCHET COLLECTION)

This 1935 photograph, probably taken in Paris by Robert Doisneau, then working for the Renault factory, shows Mlle Vera Gaulley, in a very close-fitting dress. While the effect is undeniable, you have to question the practicality of such an outfit: could she actually operate the pedals to drive this lively Reinasport cabriolet? (© PHOTOTHÈQUE RENAULT COMMUNICATION/DR)

Above: The date is 8 June 1934, and in parallel with a huge publicity campaign, the Citroën factory despatched a veritable armada to unleash its new weapon of conquest. Here two four/five seat saloons frame a two/four seat faux cabriolet in the Bois de Boulogne. At the same time in Billancourt, Renault launched a counter-offensive with the highly conventional Celtaquatre, marketed under the slogan *La voiture de l'expérience* (the car of proven experience) to cock a snook at the avant-garde nature of the creations of Citroën. In December 1934 the authorities suggested that Renault should purchase the bankrupt Citroën company for around 800 million francs, but the banks that were approached rejected this takeover.

(© PHOTOTHÈQUE CITROËN COMMUNICATION/DR)

Opposite, above: By common agreement, nowadays the Traction Avant Type 7 (two/four-seat) and Type 11 (three/five seat) cabriolets are, strictly in terms of form, thought to be the most successful series-produced cars of the mid-1930s. Flaminio Bertoni is said to have created the shape overnight in plasticene. This light-coloured drophead was registered for the first time on 28 May 1934 in Paris. The wooden barriers keeping back the spectators in the Bois de Boulogne were used at just about every concours d'élégance.

(© PHOTOTHÈQUE CITROËN COMMUNICATION/DR)

The celebrated Belgian-born actress Madeleine Ozeray was photographed at the wheel of a Renault Viva Grand Sport drophead cabriolet in the Bois de Boulogne by Robert Doisneau on 7 June 1935. That year she completed a full-length film entitled *Sous les Griffes* (*Under the Claws*) directed by Christian Jacques.

The appearance of this three-position drophead by Letourneur & Marchand on a short-chassis Delage D8-15 would certainly have aroused murmurs of admiration at the Vichy concours d'élégance in 1934. A development of the 'YoYo' line with a flowing tail and spatted rear wheels enhanced with a chrome flame, the car was finished all in white, with white leather trim, polar bear rugs, a white top and whitewall tyres. As well as at Vichy, this wonderful car won that year's concours at Paris, Aix-les-Bains, Le Touquet and Ostend. (© MUSÉE DE L'OPÉRA DE VICHY)

The catchphrase of this little Fiat Balilla 6 CV roadster at the *Fémina-L'Intransigeant* concours d'élégance organised in the Bois de Boulogne in June 1934 was 'working class but flirty'. Certainly the Comtesse Bertier de Sauvigny felt no shame in taking the controls of a car of such humble lineage. Moreover, she won the first Grand Prix d'Honneur of the meeting.

(© GILLES BLANCHET COLLECTION)

Here's another Berliet from Lyon making one of the marque's rare appearances in a concours. This is a 9 CV 944 Type VILDX-9 roadster, and in contrast with the first model of October 1933, this car has replaced the cycle wings with a more conventional skirted style. (© GILLES BLANCHET COLLECTION)

At the 1934 edition of the *Fémina-L'Intransigeant* concours d'élégance, Mme Normand has no hesitation in sitting astride the wing of her Renault Nervasport cabriolet, whose sturdy construction easily bears the featherweight young lady. First registered in the Seine département in January 1934, the car is fitted with stylish chrome wire wheels. (© PHOTOTHÈQUE RENAULT COMMUNICATION/DR)

Panhard's 'Panoramique' style was born in the spring of 1934 when the company placed a little curved glass pane on either side of the windscreen. Here at the concours d'élégance in Vichy is a five-seater four-light saloon, a model also available in six-light configuration. The little metal plaque under the bonnet reveals that this is an 'own-make' body built in the old Delaugère-Clayette car factory in Orléans, bought by Panhard in 1926 for body manufacture.

(© MUSÉE DE L'OPÉRA DE VICHY)

'Sheer presence' is the only way of describing this combination of a straight-six sleeve-valve Panhard 6CS RL-N Belka 'Panoramique' faux cabriolet with the wife of the famous illustrator Alexis Kow. The lady is dressed in a pale blue outfit by Maggy Rouf that matches the colour scheme of her car and is accompanied by her faithful black-and-white collie. In the foreground is a Panhard pedal car by Eureka, destined for the pampered children of rich parents. The first example of this wonderful toy was presented to the five-year-old son of the Sultan of Morocco, the future King Hassan II, in the Panhard showrooms on the Champs-Elysées.

(© MUSÉE DE L'OPÉRA DE VICHY)

Above: At the Paris salon of October 1933, Chenard & Walcker had given a glimpse into the future with the streamlined Mistral saloon, but the daring project was stillborn. This more conventional four-seater Chenard & Walcker steel saloon, registered in the Seine département in April 1934, has an attractive profile thanks to its low roofline. The louvres in the bonnet sides are a non-standard feature; the standard bonnets had opening vents, four on the cheaper 9 CV Aiglon range, five on the four-cylinder, six-cylinder and V8 Aigle models.

(© GILLES BLANCHET COLLECTION)

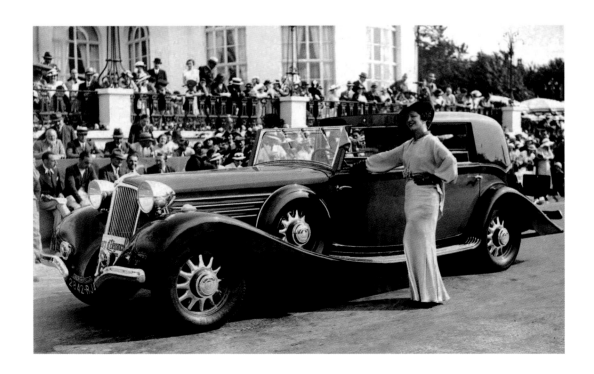

If the lines drafted by the eccentric Louis Bionier, Panhard chief designer from 1927, for the firm's catalogue models give an impression of bulk, at the same time they emanate an undeniable elegance, even as closed cars. In 1934, this Parisian manufacturer was almost alone in still retaining sleeve-valve engines which, though silent and flexible, were demanding to maintain. These engines were available in two versions: six-cylinders with a power range from 65 to 125 hp and straight-eights with an output of 130 hp.

(© GILLES BLANCHET COLLECTION)

Opposite: In 1935 the highly fashionable seaside resort of Deauville was the ideal environment to present this Renault Nervastella coupé de ville in the charming company of Mlle Jacqueline Leclerc. The imposing Nervastella chassis was only available as standard with a somewhat severe five/seven seater limousine body.

(© PHOTOTHÈQUE RENAULT COMMUNICATION/DR)

1935 RENAULT NERVASTELLA COUPÉ DE VILLE WITH EXTRAVAGANT FERNANDEZ AND DARRIN COACHWORK

Both gifted designers, the Americans Thomas L. Hibbard and Howard 'Dutch' Darrin had proved their brilliance in designing bodywork on quality chassis in their native country before setting up in business as Hibbard & Darrin in Paris in March 1923. Hibbard, who had founded the LeBaron coachworks in 1921, was French-speaking, adventurous and eager to explore a new market with great possibilities; Darrin, who had served in France during the War, loved the country. Both Hibbard and Darrin appreciated the spirit of the concours d'élégance that gave them the right milieu to display their audacious designs to best advantage.

Hiring a showroom just off the Champs-Élysées, they took over the distribution of the Belgian Minerva cars in France as the first step in their mission to create custom bodywork. Their clients included King Alfonso XIII of Spain, Lord Louis Mountbatten, the bankers Lazard Frères, the Bolivian steel magnate Patino, film star Marion Davies and a host of elite clients including diplomats, politicians, actors and financiers. The two designers participated in all the fashionable car meets: Nice, Cannes, Monte Carlo and Paris, winning many medals and prizes.

In autumn 1931 Hibbard, wearying of custom coachbuilding, was offered a salaried job with General Motors and returned to the United States, where he joined General Motors' Art & Colour Section under Harley Earl. Remaining in Paris, Darrin met a South American banker named Fernandez who was passionate about car styling and provided Darrin with both encouragement and an unexpected source of finance. The new Fernandez & Darrin coachworks at Boulogne-Billancourt created stunning bodies on Mercedes-Benz, Rolls-Royce, Voisin, Maybach, Duesenberg, Bentley, Delage, Bugatti, Hispano-Suiza, Isotta-Fraschini and even Renault chassis. In 1935 Darrin wrote a distinguished chapter in Renault history with a town car on the straight-eight Nervastella chassis, one of the most radical models ever built by the Billancourt manufacturer.

A chauffeur in a white coat with a velvet collar, cap set four-square on his head, manoeuvres the heavy Nervastella with its shiny aluminium spoked wheels into place alongside a Model J Duesenberg on the beach at Biarritz in 1935. In March of that year production of the 4825cc straight-eight Nervastella ZD 4 range ceased and a new Nervastella ACS 1 series with a 5440cc engine developing 110 hp at 2800 rpm was introduced.
(© PHOTOTHÈQUE RENAULT COMMUNICATION/DR)

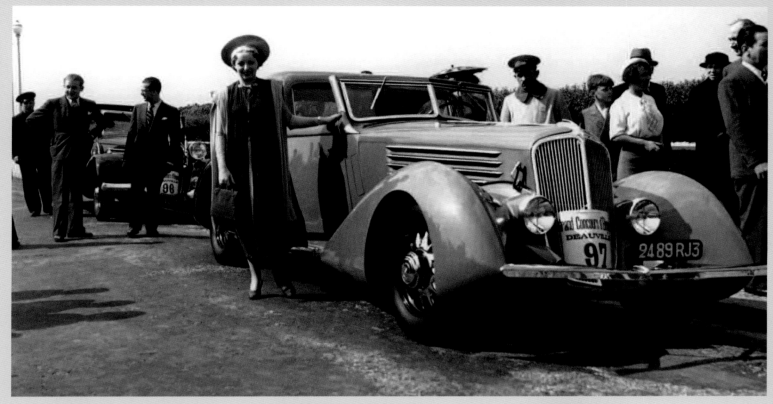

It's 8 July 1935 and this flagship model with teardrop wings and integral headlamps is graced by the presence of the Baronne de Beaufort at the Deauville concours. The registration plate indicates that the car was first put on the road on 4 September 1934 in the Seine département. In 1937 Dutch Darrin also returned to the USA, opening a bodyshop on Sunset Strip in Hollywood where he introduced the European style and created four new types for Packard.

(© PHOTOTHÈQUE RENAULT COMMUNICATION/DR)

Still in 1935, but at the fashionable seaside resort of Le Touquet in Normandy, this view of the Renault shows the formidable overhang of the teardrop front wings. The bonnet vents enhanced by chrome beadings are identical to those on the production Nervastellas.

(© PHOTOTHÈQUE RENAULT COMMUNICATION/DR)

Above: Descended from the Brougham horse-drawn carriage originally created in 1838 for the Lord Chancellor, Lord Brougham and Vaux, to use in London, the town car or coupé de ville – which here has adopted an extravagant silhouette – was normally an austere, even severe, body style. The raked windscreen and streamlined passenger compartment are highly original. When this photograph was taken, the car had been fitted with chromed wire wheels, as seen on some Nervasports, and whitewall tyres.

(© GILLES BLANCHET COLLECTION)

In the Spring of 1934, Peugeot launched the new '601' range, its first six-cylinder for three years, with a 2148cc, 60 hp, power unit. It opened new horizons for the Sochaux firm, both in commercial and image terms. Though it was strictly a production model, the roadster version with its fold-down windscreen – only available in the 'Normale' range with a wheelbase of 9 ft 9 in – revealed itself as a very attractive car, often admired at car meets. At that time the absence of running boards was a sign of modernity. On the other hand, the steel cover for the spare wheel, with its stainless steel clasp, was a sure sign of attention to detail. (© GILLES BLANCHET COLLECTION)

Made to order, the Renault Nerva Grand Sport – this example was photographed during a meeting at Cabourg on 15 August 1937 – was a dauntingly large car with a most unusual shape. Despite a reaction that was sometimes lukewarm, throughout his career Louis Renault tried to offer cars at the upper end of the market, in this case an enormous straight-eight of 5448cc developing 110 hp. This roadster with a fold-flat windscreen cost a hefty 55,000 francs, while a humble Celtaquatre could be bought for just 16,500 francs. (© PHOTOTHÈQUE RENAULT COMMUNICATION/DR)

In October 1932 Citroën began production of the new '15', which replaced the C6 G; its 15
CV engine developed 56 hp at 3200 rpm. This two-tone 'cabriolet-roadster' with its
folding windscreen is one of the company's *hors-série* range bodied by outside
coachbuilders like SICAL, Manessius or Million-Guiet, but sold at an affordable price. In
1933 there were 52 models in this series, available on all five chassis in the Citroën range.

(© PHOTOTHÈQUE CITROËN COMMUNICATION/DR)

On 28 June 1935, Jacqueline Delubac, the third wife of playwright and film director Sacha Guitry –
at 50, 22 years her senior – showed this 31 CV Renault Nerva Grand Sport with 'hyper-
aérodynamique' two-tone cabriolet bodywork at the *Fémina-L'Intransigeant* concours d'élégance.
She starred in eleven of Guitry's films, and had just completed filming *Bonne Chance!* (*Good Luck!*)
in which she played a little Parisian washerwoman who becomes a wealthy lady.

Also unveiled at the Paris Salon in October 1934 was this striking novelty from the French Talbot company, the 'Baby Sport'. It was another step forward for the old-established firm that was in the process of rebirth. The long, low lines evoke the British SS saloon, predecessor of the Jaguar, designed by William Lyons. That was a car which Tony Lago, who had taken over the Suresnes company, enthusiastically admired. (© GILLES BLANCHET COLLECTION)

For the 1935 season, the standard bodies offered on the Type 57 Bugatti chassis were the Galibier saloon, the Ventoux coupé and this cabriolet, the Stelvio. From this angle, its wood-framed steel-panelled body has a rather heavy look at the rear. That couldn't be said about the magnificent roadster also built on a Type 57 chassis designed by young Jean Bugatti, the son of 'Le Patron' Ettore Bugatti, shown on the firm's stand at the October 1934 Paris Salon. With the evocative name of 'Grand Raid', this sportster with streamlined head-rests never passed the prototype stage.

(© GILLES BLANCHET COLLECTION)

'Spectacular' is the only word to describe the berlinette built on a specially-prepared Delage D8-120 Grand Sport short chassis by the master craftsmen of Figoni & Falaschi. Powered by a tuned 3-litre straight-six developing 120 hp and intended to compete in the 1936 Le Mans 24-hour race (which was cancelled because of the wave of strikes that affected France that year), the car was originally painted orange, then vermilion. The opening rear panel gave access to a dickey seat that could accommodate two extra passengers for short distances. The car carried off the Grand Prix des Voitures Aérodynamiques in the concours d'élégance organised by the journal *L'Auto* on 26 June 1936. (© GILLES BLANCHET COLLECTION)

Back seat drivers

Essential partners at the most highly-respected concours d'élégance, always well-disciplined and responding to the slightest movements or commands of their mistresses, the dogs had impeccable pedigrees and were endowed with impressive names that reflected the image of their adoptive families.
(© GILLES BLANCHET COLLECTION)

The 1935 vintage Talbot Baby Sport was available as a four-seat tourer as well as a saloon, and had bolt-on wire wheels with chromed hubcaps rather than the Rudge-type knock-off hubs fitted to the T150 Grand Sport. The Baby's 2996cc ohv straight-six developed 90 hp at 3800 rpm. Its price was 52,000 francs in 1935, the year that Tony Lago purchased Automobiles Talbot for the equivalent of £63,000. (© GILLES BLANCHET COLLECTION)

In July 1937 this 18 CV Delahaye type 135 Sport bodied by Henri Chapron carried off the Prix d'Honneur awarded by the jury at the concours d'élégance held in Deauville. Praiseworthy on this three-position drophead were the alternately convex and concave semi-circular bonnet vents and the thin-bladed bumper with over-riders, very different from the thick-bladed bumper seen at the beginning of the 1937 season. The slender wire wheels with knock-off hubs were not fitted on the entry-level Types 134 (12 CV) and 148 (20 CV) offered by this marque from the Rue du Banquier in Paris.

(© GILLES BLANCHET COLLECTION)

Above: The '20 CV' script on the radiator of this Delahaye, registered in the Seine département on 20 March 1937, shows that it has a 3557cc six-cylinder engine, a power unit fitted to the Type 148 launched in July 1936 (though this model was fitted with bolt-on wire wheels and didn't have the thin-bladed bumper with over-riders) and the long chassis Type 135 C introduced at the 1935 Paris Salon. What is certain is that this handsome drophead coupé was built outside the Delahaye factory, probably by Henri Chapron.

(© GILLES BLANCHET COLLECTION)

Opposite, top: This photograph proves that a modest 8 CV Peugeot 301 CR is quite able to hold its own among the big boys at the top meets, as here at the concours d'élégance in the Jardin d'Acclimation in June 1934. The small oval plaque at the base of the coachwork appears to be that of the coachbuilder Meulemeester Frères of Clichy.

(© GILLES BLANCHET COLLECTION)

Opposite, below: It would take the skills of a Sherlock Holmes to discover the identity of this flower-bedecked participant in the concours d'élégance at Vichy, though the twin rear wheels would seem to indicate a commercial vehicle rather than a private car. The organisers of the Vichy concours were insistent on their participation as they recalled the traditional 'flower battles' seen at carnivals in the past.

(© MUSÉE DE L'OPÉRA DE VICHY)

The six-cylinder engines which equipped Renault's 1935 Vivasport range like this four/five seat convertible were originally 21 CV units of 3620cc, developing 80 hp (Type YZ 4) but from 26 March 1935 an increase in bore from 80 to 85 mm brought the engine into the 23 CV taxation class and increased the displacement to 4086cc (Type ACM 1), with an output of 85 hp. On the appearance front, the 1935 Renaults adopted horizontal bonnet vents and spoked wheels, which, despite their subtle decoration, looked somewhat conservative for the period. But then Renault's philosophy was one of continuity rather than dramatic change. (© GILLES BLANCHET COLLECTION)

Opposite: This imposing Panhard 6CS-Vulma 16 CV five-seater saloon would have definitely commanded respect on the highways and urban streets of 1935. The bouquet affixed at the base of the windscreen would indicate that it has won a class award at this summertime concours. The flared legs of the girl's beach pyjamas and the man's polo shirt represent the height of fashionable elegance at the smart resorts.

(© GILLES BLANCHET COLLECTION)

It was natural that the top-of-the-range Aigle 8 should represent the Chenard & Walcker company in concours d'élégance. Shown at the concours organised by the daily *L'Auto* in June 1937, this cabriolet by the coachbuilder Labarre of Evreux has a rather prominent rear boot and is less successful aesthetically than the catalogue version. The car is powered by the firm's own 3.6-litre V8 engine: of the other French makers, only Matford used a similar configuration that year.

(© GILLES BLANCHET COLLECTION)

The dashingly sporty lines of the roadster from the Georges Irat range always did well at concours meets. This 1937 season Georges Irat has a Ruby engine beneath its bonnet driving the front wheels through a three-speed transmission. A car like this would normally only wear Dunlop 130×40 whitewall tyres at this kind of fashionable competition. (© GILLES BLANCHET COLLECTION)

Alongside its regular contracts, the Franay firm of Levallois-Perret specialised in building coupé de ville bodywork on top-quality French and foreign chassis, like this 1937 vintage Delage D8-100, registered on 1 February 1937 in the Seine département. As the journalist Charles Faroux remarked: 'Delages are the cars that wear fine coachwork the best.'

(© GILLES BLANCHET COLLECTION)

On the fine summer's morning of 25 June 1937, Andrée Berty – who appeared that year in the acclaimed film, *Les Filles du Rhône*, drove before the jury of the concours organised by the daily *L'Intransigeant* at the wheel of a Renault Nerva Grand Sport bodied by Figoni. Its custom radiator shell means that only the diamond-shaped radiator badge identifies this sporty roadster with a fold-flat windscreen as a Renault.

(© PHOTOTHÈQUE RENAULT COMMUNICATION/DR)

The 3-litre Talbot Baby Sport 17 CV, launched at the October 1934 Paris Salon, is seen here in July 1936 at the concours d'élégance in the Bois de Boulogne, accompanied by the charming Nina Ricci, who had founded her own design house in 1932 at the age of 49. The elegant two-tone roadster carried off the Grand Prix for convertibles with factory bodywork. (© GILLES BLANCHET COLLECTION)

After winning the Coupe des Dames in the 1937 du Rallye du Maroc, the flowing lines of this roadster created by the panel-beaters of the Letourneur & Marchand bodyshop on a 16 CV Delage D6-70 were displayed at many meets. Its long (10 ft 11 in) wheelbase doesn't seem well-suited to this style of sporting bodywork. (© GILLES BLANCHET COLLECTION)

At the *Fémina* concours d'élégance of 25 June 1937, Claude May strikes a pose alongside the most expensive Renault convertible, the Nerva Grand Sport 31 CV type ABM-7 three-seater with dickey, of which just 22 examples were built, plus an equal number of six-seat convertibles, out of a total output of 104 Nerva Grand Sports. Despite a weight of 1.85 tons, its 5448cc straight-eight engine gave a creditable top speed of 90 mph.

(© PHOTOTHÈQUE RENAULT COMMUNICATION/DR)

Let's be honest, while the body by Gangloff of Colmar, so representative of the style created by Ettore Bugatti and his son Jean, can be considered as a hymn in praise of suppleness and sensuality, the lady's dress, with its fancy flounces and over-elaborate pattern of multicoloured dots, is hardly in keeping! This ill-matched ensemble was seen at the Auteuil meeting in the summer of 1937.

(© GILLES BLANCHET COLLECTION)

Whilst concentrating on feminine elegance at the concours events, the notion of elegance as a way of life was well established, and smart gentlemen were not going to be left out. As with cars, concours d'élégance held up a mirror to the latest fashion trends. The natty gent on the right is wearing a three-button flannel suit with a Prince of Wales check, and the outfit is completed by a hand-stitched camelhair sports overcoat with a half-belt. The cane may not be necessary, given his relative youth, but it undeniably adds a touch of distinction.

(PATRICK LESUEUR COLLECTION)

The young lady seems rather too formally dressed for this smart cabriolet on a 1937 Licorne 8 CV Type CL-415, with coachwork by Duval of Boulogne-sur-Seine, a regular supplier of bodies to the Courbevoie firm. Given the short (9 ft 4 in) wheelbase of the Licorne, it's a well-proportioned body with a contrasting and noteworthy flash on the door.

(© GILLES BLANCHET COLLECTION)

N° 93

AUTOMOBILE ET TOURISME

Le Numéro : **3** fr.

Mai 1936

SUR LA CÔTE D'AZUR

cassarini

The cover of the monthly *Automobile et Tourisme* for May 1936 reflects the spirit of a year that saw the signing of the Matignon Accords, which gave France's workers – who had struck for better conditions – a fortnight's paid holiday, higher wages and a 40-hour week. If car ownership was still an impossible dream for most Frenchmen, this magazine openly encouraged those who did have cars to flee the towns and cities and holiday in the countryside, the mountains or beside the sea.

(© GILLES BLANCHET COLLECTION)

Styled by the talented designer Georges Paulin for the coachbuilder Pourtout of Rueil-Malmaison, this roadster seen in the Place du Trocadéro in Paris on 23 June1939 must be one of the prettiest bodies of the year, yet beneath its sleek lines is the humble chassis of a Renault Primaquatre. Apparently 24 examples of this model were built between March and September 1939 with the help of Renault's subsidiary SAPRAR. (© PHOTOTHÈQUE RENAULT COMMUNICATION/DR)

From the early 1930s, the so-called golfing outfit with its plus-fours, Fair Isle pullover and cheese-cutter cap had been a favourite with amateur sportsmen and enthusiastic drivers. Even though this was considered a sporting outfit, of course a tie was essential, and not to wear two-tone 'co-respondent' shoes would have been considered bad form. The artist who created this advertisement for Olympic suitings ('Made in England') has decided that this fashionable chap has arrived at his favourite golf club at the wheel of a low-slung Bucciali TAV 30 cabriolet, an excellent (though quite impractical as the TAV 30 was only a mock-up) choice of car to impress his fellow golfers. (PATRICK LESUEUR COLLECTION)

Seen from behind, the lines of the Renault Primaquatre Sport roadster are frankly sexy, with the fully-enclosed wheels contributing considerably to the fluid lines of the bodywork. However, under the skin, the chassis is far less seductive: it's a strictly standard 2383cc four-cylinder sidevalve developing 56 hp at 3300 rpm. (© PHOTOTHÈQUE RENAULT COMMUNICATION/DR)

Besides the roadster with its cutaway doors, the Primaquatre Sport was also available as a drophead coupé body with a fixed windscreen and conventional doors. At the wheel is Geneviève Boucher de la Bruyère, the aristocratic wife of fashion designer Jacques Fath; she was a former model who had once been Coco Chanel's secretary. (© PHOTOTHÈQUE RENAULT COMMUNICATION/DR)

Taking its style from America – then the world's most innovative source of design – the Rosengart Supertraction Type LR 539 unveiled to the press in February 1939 was a real success in terms of shape, and regularly won top concours awards. The two-tone paint finish and faired-in headlamps are distinctive features of this three-position drophead, whose front-wheel drive is courtesy of a Citroën 11 CV drivetrain. (© PHOTOTHÈQUE RENAULT COMMUNICATION/DR)

Despite its humble parentage, this Simca-Huit cabriolet, with whitewall tyres and – the ultimate irony – a chauffeur in full dress , is taking part in the Trocadéro meeting of June 1939. Under the stubby bonnet is a four-cylinder 1090cc engine with overhead valves developing a modest 32 hp. (© PHOTOTHÈQUE RENAULT COMMUNICATION/DR)

The Renault Viva Grand Sport drophead convertible of 1937 was a full six-seater, enabling its occupants to take the air in great comfort. The elegant vee-radiator and built-in headlamps in teardop housings have a definite transatlantic air, giving a distinctive personality to this flagship model from Billancourt. The car is shown by the slender Raya Dembo, doubtless a starlet of the day, whose fame has proved transient. (© PHOTOTHÈQUE RENAULT COMMUNICATION/DR)

On the same occasion, a fleet of Simca 5 Découvrables Grand Luxe lines up alongside its big sister, the Simca 8. While whitewall tyres were essential wear on such occasions, they were rarely seen in normal use.
(PHOTOTHÈQUE RENAULT COMMUNICATION/DR)

One of the handsomest Renaults ever produced – at least, in the author's opinion – is this three-seater convertible and dickey on the Suprastella 31 CV straight-eight chassis, here entrusted to the actress Colette Clauday for the *Fémina-L'Intransigeant* concours d'élégance held on 23 June 1939 at the foot of the Palais de Chaillot. The Suprastella ABM 8 was the absolute pinnacle of prestige for Renault; just 24 were built between April 1938 and July 1939, of which only seven were drophead three-seaters. (© PHOTOTHÈQUE RENAULT COMMUNICATION/DR)

What the smart motorist was wearing in the late 1930s: these two outfits reflect the lack of heating in the cars of the day. On the left is a pin-striped suit in thick flannel, while on the right is a three-button double-breasted tweed suit with long lapels; the cloth was warm, comfortable and pleasant to wear. It's accompanied by a gabardine raincoat , driving gloves and – of course – the felt hat without which no smart gentleman would leave the house.

(PATRICK LESUEUR COLLECTION)

THE RENAULT JUVAQUATRE AT THE CONCOURS D'ÉLÉGANCE

A POPULAR CAR ON PARADE

Under the soaring glass roof of the Grand Palais in Paris, where the 1937 Salon de l'Automobile took place from Thursday 7 to Sunday 17 October, a crowd of eager onlookers milled around the Renault stand, where a brand new 6 CV model was on display. Known as the Type AEB 2 Juvaquatre, the latest star from the Renault factory on the Ile Seguin broke new ground for the company: it was the first Renault with unitary body/chassis and independent front suspension; a couple of years later, in November 1939, this model would pioneer another break with Renault tradition by becoming the Billancourt company's first model with hydraulic braking. On the styling front, the Juvaquatre was distinguished by its headlamps, which were carried in fairings integrated into the bonnet like the Opel Olympia, which Louis Renault had admired at the Berlin Show in February 1935. The career of the Juvaquatre saloon would continue after the war as the only Renault private car available until the launch of the 4 CV; production would finish at the end of the 1948 season. The new Juvaquatre would be the proud torch bearer for the mass market Renaults alongside more expensive models. In short, a great image of industrial diversity.

Taken outside the Palais de Chaillot on 24 June 1938, this photograph shows Miss Paris alongside a Juvaquatre 'Grand Luxe', distinguished by twin horns behind the radiator grille and the front bumper. Few private owners would have specified whitewall tyres. The lines of the car have a certain equilibrium, unlike the lady's bonnet!
(© PHOTOTHÈQUE RENAULT COMMUNICATION/DR)

This picture, taken the same day, shows a charming hors-concours group was entitled 'Snow White and the Seven Dwarfs' in homage to the feature-length Walt Disney cartoon released in 1937, a few months before this photograph was taken; the Juvaquatre was registered in the Seine département on 25 May 1938.

(© PHOTOTHÈQUE RENAULT COMMUNICATION/DR)

On 30 March 1939, Renault unveiled this Juvaquatre soft-top saloon built by Renault's SAPRAR division. This car has a non-standard metallic finish and chrome rimbellishers , a turnout perfectly in accord with the spirit of this sort of joyously elegant occasion. (© PHOTOTHÈQUE RENAULT COMMUNICATION/DR)

The launch of its Grand Luxe coupé version on 30 May 1939 was a significant date for the Juvaquatre. Its chunky, flowing lines, crowned by the rounded roofline, give it a reassuring appeal, rather more sexy than the young Micheline Presle — then aged only 18 — who presented No 58 with its unusual pale paint finish, at the concours. That year the young actress appeared alongside Fernand Gravey in the film *Le Paradis Perdu* (*Paradise Lost*), directed by the great Abel Gance.

(© PHOTOTHÈQUE RENAULT COMMUNICATION/DR)

The charming Jacqueline Monteran was given the task of presenting this two-door Juvaquatre with its daring two-tone colour scheme. If Renault's publicity department was keen to show the Juvaquatre at such fashionable meets, there was a very good reason for promoting the little saloon, for its sales were disappointing. Louis Renault attributed this poor performance to the fact that only a two-door version was offered, but a four-door Juvaquatre, the Type ABB 3, did not become available until 15 May 1939. (© PHOTOTHÈQUE RENAULT COMMUNICATION/DR)

This little would-be mannequin poses proudly alongside a Juvaquatre AEB 2 coupé at the Deauville concours d'élégance in the summer of 1939. This is a top-of-the range model, distinguishable by its three-spoke ivory-coloured steering wheel and over-riders: some examples destined for concours events, like this car, first registered in the Seine département on 10 June 1939, were fitted with chrome-plated steel wheels.

(© PHOTOTHÈQUE RENAULT COMMUNICATION/DR)

Oddly enough, French coachbuilders rarely seemed fully at ease when it came to bodying American chassis, and their work often lacked the light touch of their opposite numbers in the USA. However, that wasn't the case with this Packard Super Eight cabriolet, bodied in the shops of Franay in Levallois-Perret during 1939. That year the Detroit company finally ceased production of its prestigious V12 range, which had been unveiled at the 1932 New York Show. It's just a shame that the spectator in the hat has obscured the car's tail, which seems to end in a point, speedster fashion. (© GILLES BLANCHET COLLECTION)

For 1938-39, the Suprastella's headlights – in common with the Viva Grand Sport and Vivastella – were mounted in streamlined pods atop the front wings. This six-light, eight-seater limousine is a rare version with an extra-long (12 ft 2 in) wheelbase of which just ten were built. One notable customer for the Suprastella was playwright and film director Sacha Guitry; the limousine with division, which he had ordered at the 1938 Paris Salon, was delivered on 18 April 1939. It was green, with matching leather in the chauffeur's compartment and cloth trim in the rear, and had a radio.

(© PHOTOTHÈQUE RENAULT COMMUNICATION/DR)

A large crowd gathered at Auteuil on 9 June 1939 to observe the concours d'élégance organised by the daily newspaper *L'Auto*. In the foregound, behind the faded chalk line indicating its place in the line-up, is a Delahaye 135 M two-seater fixed-head coupé by Henri Chapron with unusually skinny front bumpers; the crowd seems to be ignoring it. Behind it stands a majestic 1939 Cadillac coupé de ville, almost certainly bodied in France. (© GILLES BLANCHET COLLECTION)

One of Italy's premier concours was held in Turin's Valentino Park; the winning car in the open sports car category in the X Concorso di Eleganza del Valentino of 2 June 1939 was this lithe 'spider sport 2 posti' built on an Alfa Romeo 8C2900 B chassis to the order of Count Salvi del Pero by the master panelbeaters of Pinin Farina. All-metal framing increased the body's rigidity. Its teardrop wings subtly enfold the wheels to enhance the fluid lines of the ensemble. (© GILLES BLANCHET COLLECTION)

These two sketches by William Rossi were published in an Italian motor magazine in 1935 and reveal the styling trends anticipated for the 1940s. However, they don't feature the pontoon wings that would be the dominant modernist trend in coachwork design. The fascinating lines of the coupé de ville, with its streamlined cockpit, are nevertheless worthy of admiration.

(© GILLES BLANCHET COLLECTION)

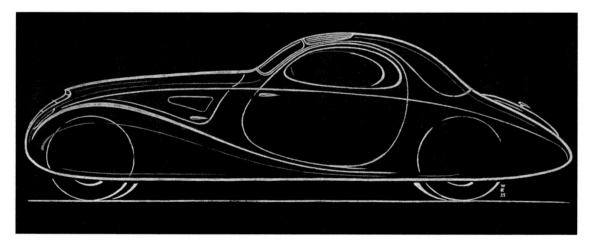

When this photo was taken in 1939, the young Swiss actress Annie Vernay, perched elegantly on the bonnet of a Model J Duesenberg, was the rising star of French cinema. Two years later, on 18 August 1941, she was dead, struck down by typhoid fever while visiting Buenos Aires; she was not yet 20. In 1939 she starred in three full-length films: *Les Otages*, produced by Raymond Bernard, *Chantons quand même*, produced by Pierre Caron and *Dédé la musique*, produced by André Berthomieu. The choice of a Duesenberg – possibly the four-door berline by Franay that had appeared at the Jardin d'Acclimation concours in 1934 – is interesting, as the Indianapolis marque had ceased production two years earlier. (PATRICK LESUEUR COLLECTION)

FROM AUSTERITY TO FINS AND CHROME

IN THE IMMEDIATE POSTWAR PERIOD, FRANCE HAD AN OVER-RIDING PRIORITY: THE RECONSTRUCTION OF A SHATTERED COUNTRY. WAS THERE STILL A PLACE FOR THE SORT OF SPECTACLE THAT WAS CONSIDERED OSTENTATIOUS – AND EVEN RATHER FRIVOLOUS? AS HAD BEEN THE CASE 27 YEARS EARLIER, CONCOURS D'ELEGANCE WERE REVIVED TO SATISFY THE FERVENT NEED FOR RECOVERING A CERTAIN SERENITY – AND, WHY NOT, A HINT OF PLEASURE WITH A DASH OF SAUCINESS. NEVERTHELESS, THE CAST OF THESE PARADES WAS GRADUALLY CHANGING AS ONE BY ONE THE GREAT COACHBUILDERS CLOSED THEIR DOORS. MADE-TO-MEASURE CARS WERE REPLACED BY MACHINES MORE CLOSELY RELATED TO EVERYDAY PRODUCTION. AFTER THE SOCIAL TURMOIL IN FRANCE DURING 1968, THE CHANGING ATTITUDES IT TRIGGERED SAW THE GRADUAL DISAPPEARANCE OF THE OLD-STYLE CONCOURS.

Built by Franay for the 1946 Paris Salon on a 1937 Delahaye Type 145 competition chassis powered by a V12 engine, this spectacularly baroque roadster was presented at the Palais de Chaillot Concours d'Élégance in 1947 by the Comtesse de Pouget. This particularly exuberant exercise by Marius Franay reveals an inspiration similar to that of his fellow coachbuilders Figoni & Falaschi or Saoutchik. Only five chassis of this competition model were built, plus four or five examples of the road-going Type 165 V12. (© GILLES BLANCHET COLLECTION)

Not every car entered for postwar concours d'élégance was of noble lineage, for times were hard. In evidence, this humble Renault Primaquatre cabriolet, registered in the Seine département in August 1939, appears in this photo taken at the La Baule concours of 19 August 1949. In the background is a Peugeot 202, another car of equally modest parentage. (© GILLES BLANCHET COLLECTION)

Simone Chapron, daughter of the famous coachbuilder – who had founded his company in Neuilly-sur-Seine in 1920 to build bodies for Model T Fords – poses beside a lovely two-tone Delahaye type 135 MS drophead. The banner on the door reveals that the car has won the Grand Prix d'Excellence at the 1947 concours d'élégance of Paris, held at the foot of the Grande Cascade in the Bois de Boulogne. (© GILLES BLANCHET COLLECTION)

In those dismal postwar years of reconstruction, America was seen as the promised land, thrusting and modern, and this 1947 Buick Roadmaster Series 70 Model 47-76C cabriolet is a magnificent symbol of that spirit. Powered by a 4-litre straight-eight developing 144 hp, it is very well-finished for a basically standard production car, with electro-hydraulic operation of the seats and windows. On the other hand, the telephone didn't appear in the catalogue, even as an option!
(© GILLES BLANCHET COLLECTION)

A transatlantic product that didn't feature in postwar concours d'élégance was the Chrysler New Yorker Town and Country, of which only 3309 examples were built during 1948. It's a pity, because this modern interpretation of the 'woodie' body with its Honduras mahogany panels framed in ash – a structure that was both functional and decorative – would certainly have carried off many prizes.
(© GILLES BLANCHET COLLECTION)

Concours d'élégance were often combined with other events, like the election of 'Miss Europe', in this case Miss Poland, whose charms enhance the commanding presence of this 1948 DeSoto Custom Series cabriolet. Dominating the front of the car is its aggressive chromed 'mouthorgan' grille, behind whose vertical slats is a sidevalve straight six of 3890cc with a power output of 109 hp.

(© GILLES BLANCHET COLLECTION)

It's difficult to imagine a more iconoclastic body style than the 'Narval' introduced by Figoni & Falaschi at the 1946 Paris salon, with its protuberant 'nose' above the radiator grille. Nevertheless, a Narval owned by Annie Verrières won the 1947 'Miss Automobile' contest and high-profile owners like popular singer Charles Trénet and Prince Aly Khan bought Narvals. Incidentally, the total 1947 output of the Delahaye-Delage combine was only 380 cars. (© GILLES BLANCHET COLLECTION)

Figoni's *pièce de résistance* at the 1948 Paris Salon was this elegantly restrained fixed-head coupé finished in a golden shade, with bright work gold-plated by the 'Dalic process'. Inside, the trim was suede leather, with lambswool carpets on the floor. The firm also showed 'an elaborate and enormously long' roadster on the Delahaye stand that featured a Michelin Guide which had cost 40,000 francs to bind in ivory. (© GILLES BLANCHET COLLECTION)

Painted in Empire Blue, this 26 CV Talbot-Record 26 displayed at the 1948 Enghien concours d'élégance and registered in the Seine département in May that year, is an unusually restrained design by Saoutchik, given distinction by its narrow radiator grille. (© GILLES BLANCHET COLLECTION)

Claude Pourtout, son of the talented coachbuilder from Rueil-Malmaison, penned the flowing lines of this cabriolet body, devoid of all unnecessary decoration, on a Talbot T26 Record chassis. It won the Grand Prix d'Honneur at the 1948 Bois de Boulogne concours. Finished in Lido Green, a shade supplied by the well-known Nitrolac paint company, the car was registered in the Rhône département in January 1948.

(© GILLES BLANCHET COLLECTION)

In June 1948 the Swiss coachbuilder Graber unveiled this Talbot-Lago Record cabriolet whose rather massively-sculpted front end has such yielding lines. This evocative photograph leads one to yearn with regret for a time when elegant ladies donned gloves and wide-brimmed hats to go motoring. (© GILLES BLANCHET COLLECTION)

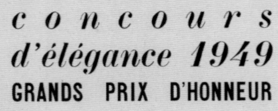

Based at 130-146 Rue Daniel-Casanova in Saint-Denis, the Nitrolac automobile paint company was a privileged partner of top-flight coachbuilders. The firm took advantage of this to insert numerous advertisements in the specialist press, like this example from 1949, to draw attention to the number of Grands Prix d'Honneur won at concours by cars finished in Nitrolac paint. (© GILLES BLANCHET COLLECTION)

The coachbuilder Antem of Courbevoie bodied this Delahaye 135 cabriolet, presented by the actress Barbara Laage (born Claire Colombat in Menthon-Saint-Bernard, Haute Savoie), at the 1948 concours d'élégance of Paris, held in front of the Pavillon d'Ermenonville in the Bois de Boulogne. The young film star carried off the Grand Prix d'Honneur for open cars of 14-20 CV as well as the cup awarded by Parfums Carven. (© GILLES BLANCHET COLLECTION)

In October 1949 the Paris Salon hosted an indoor concours d'élégance entitled 'Gala de l'Automobile' beneath the soaring ironwork of the fin de siècle Grand Palais. Marius Franay, the dedicated coachbuilder based at the Porte de Champerret in Levallois-Perret, displayed this light-coloured Bentley cabriolet beneath the spotlights.

(© GILLES BLANCHET COLLECTION)

Below: Beneath the lowering sky that hung over the Bois de Boulogne in the spring of 1948, the 'Rouge Luxe' paintwork of the recently-launched 26 CV Delahaye type 175 gleams alluringly. With a cabriolet body by the bodyshop of Jacques Saoutchik, based at 46 Rue Jacques-Dulud in Neuilly-sur-Seine, the car would enjoy success in more clement weather, winning the Grand Prix d'Honneur in the category for French cars at Nice.

(© GILLES BLANCHET COLLECTION)

Above: 'Family groups' were a favourite theme for concours d'élégance, and this photo taken at the 1949 concours organised by the spa town of Vichy is typical. Not only does it reveal the restrained elegance of the Delahaye 135 saloon, but it also pictures the three little girls, dressed all in white like their mother (real or pretended) and ranked in order of age. The car was first registered in the Seine département in 1949.

(© MUSÉE DE L'OPÉRA DE VICHY)

Born Geneviève Lucie Menut in Montmartre in 1912, the actress Ginette Leclerc (1912–1992) looks well pleased with the Delage D-6 3 Litres cabriolet bodied by Guilloré of Courbevoie (active 1937–1951) that she is presenting at the Lac d'Enghien meeting in May 1948. The young actress, who had been imprisoned for a year after the Liberation because she had worked for the German firm Continental during the war, had just finished filming *Une Belle Garce* (*A Pretty Wench* – an all too customary role for Ginette!) under the director Jacques Daroy. Her most celebrated role was 'Denise' in the controversial 1943 film *Le Corbeau* (*The Raven*). (© GILLES BLANCHET COLLECTION)

In May 1949 the apron at Orly airport served as a backdrop to this promotional shot of the recently-introduced 3 CV Panhard Dyna 100. Seemingly painted a patriotic blue, white and red, the plebeian little saloons, built in Panhard's Porte d'Ivry (Paris) factory, are in stark contrast to the high fashion outfits of the three models. The French-built freight and passenger aeroplane is a Breguet Br.893S Mercure and was the only one made. (© GILLES BLANCHET COLLECTION)

Franay reprised the daring styling first seen on the Delahaye 145 Competition at the 1946 Paris Salon, with detail differences like the headlamp position and the chrome accents, on this 135 drophead seen at the concours d'élégance in the Place Vendôme on 17 June 1950. The car was registered in the Seine département in January 1950.

(© GILLES BLANCHET COLLECTION)

Accompanied by the inevitable lapdog, the model strikes a cheekily casual pose atop the two-door drophead. The little plaque affixed at the base of the door of this 1948 Delahaye Type 135 reveals that the body is the work of Franay. Typical of the custom-built bodies of the late 1940s are the chrome accents on the wings; the wave curling over the rear wheel spat is particularly attractive.

(© GILLES BLANCHET COLLECTION)

Unveiled in 1948, this splendid low-slung cabriolet bodied by Faget & Varnet is based on a Delahaye Type 135 chassis. This coachbuilder from Levallois-Perret, had adopted a modern '*tout acier*' (all-steel) method of construction distinctly different from the antediluvian technique of attaching metal panels over a wooden frame used by its distinguished contemporaries. (© GILLES BLANCHET COLLECTION)

Opposite page: Posed in front of the Arc de Triomphe du Carrousel, this lovely lady is presenting the new Simca 6 launched at the 1947 Salon. The Simca 6 drophead saloon had a pleasantly modern look and differed from the Simca 5 in having overhead valves. A mere 191 units would leave Simca's Nanterre factory the following year, but the economical Simca 5 remained very much in demand.
(© GILLES BLANCHET COLLECTION))

Beautiful and exotic, this two-door, two-seat, saloon, chassis number 110103, was created on a 1949 vintage Talbot Lago Grand Sport chassis by Figoni & Falaschi. Outstanding are the flowing lines of the rear end with the completely enclosed wheels and the use of the bumpers as decorative features. More aesthetically debatable is the front end treatment with its central headlamp. (PATRICK LESUEUR COLLECTION)

The editor in chief of the monthly *Réalités* magazine featured this spectacular coupé by Saoutchik on the front cover of his 1949 Salon de l'Automobile issue. It took part in several concours d'élégance that season, but it wasn't just a pretty shape. Beneath that long bonnet was a 4482 straight six with overhead valves that developed a brawny 190 hp, enabling a top speed of some 125 mph. (PATRICK LESUEUR COLLECTION)

To say that the stylists of the Franay workshops had been a trifle heavy-handed in designing this Bentley cabriolet would perhaps be an understatement, but then the bodies normally fitted to the Mk VI chassis were no lightweights. Nevertheless, this car, with a raven black Nitrolac finish, carried off the 'hors concours' class at the 1948 Enghien concours.

(© GILLES BLANCHET COLLECTION)

The Saoutchik Talbot Lago coupé takes its place on the judging stand at the presentation in the Place Vendôme in Paris on 7 June 1950. Like the great majority of quality French cars built before the mid-1950s, it has right-hand drive. One wonders how the elegant lady got on to the roof!

(© GILLES BLANCHET COLLECTION)

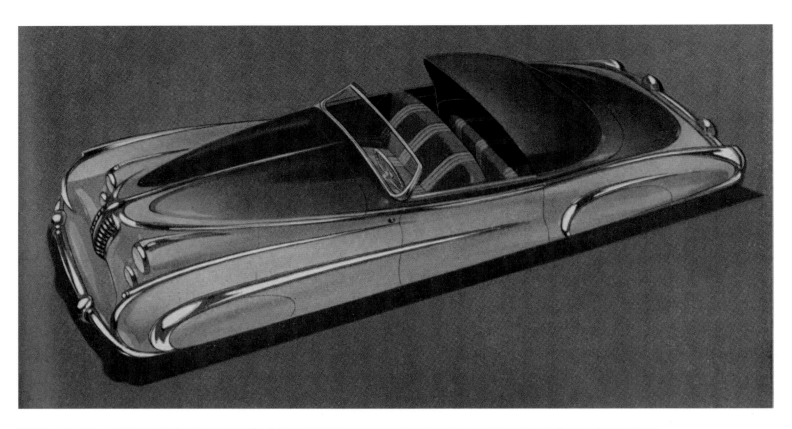

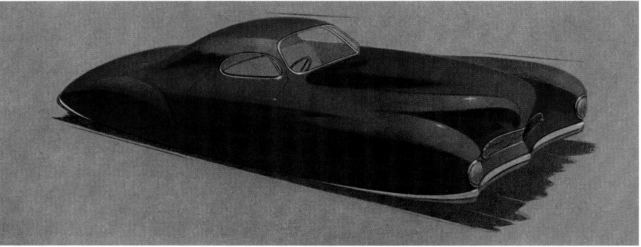

In the autumn of 1948, Baron Charles Petiet, President of the Fédération Nationale de l'Automobile, assessed the state of the industry. Concerning styling, Petiet cited three great French coachbuilders, illustrating his remarks with the famous Figoni-bodied Delahaye and two concepts, a highly-streamlined coupé by Chapron and a massive open drive Cadillac with fixed rear quarter by Saoutchik, which had all the ostentatious features dear to the heart of the Neuilly coachbuilder.

(PATRICK LESUEUR COLLECTION)

The Paris Salon sometimes used some concours style to display special cars with elegant models dressed by the great couturiers. In 1949 this Talbot T26 GS cabriolet bodied by Franay won the Grand Prix de l'Art et de l'Industrie. Its gimmicky grille has 'ears' incorporating the spotlamps.

(© GILLES BLANCHET COLLECTION)

10, RUE DU BANQUIER - PARIS

Above: The well-known industrial designer and talented illustrator Philippe Charbonneau was hired by Delahaye to design the 1948 catalogue range; the illustrations were also used for advertisements in the press, like this very elegant Type 135 MS roadster. The 'GFA' emblem represents the Générale Française Automobile, a combine formed in 1941 between the Delahaye, Delage, Simca, Unic, Laffly and Bernard companies.

(© GILLES BLANCHET COLLECTION)

Right: Concours d'élégance often benefited from the presence of popular film stars like Paulette Dubost, photographed here on 12 June 1948 at the Journées Automobiles d'Enghien. Born in 1910, Paulette Dubost began her career at the age of seven at the Paris Opera and appeared in over 250 films. One of her most famous roles was as the bubbly maid 'Lisette' in the celebrated 1939 film *La Règle du Jeu* (*Rules of the Game*), directed by the legendary Jean Renoir. 'Witty, naughty and clever', Paulette Dubost would live to be over 100.

(© GILLES BLANCHET COLLECTION)

Launched at the 1947 Paris Salon, Renault's revolutionary little rear-engined 760cc 4 CV
was being produced at the rate of 175 units a day from November 1948 and, despite its
unsophisticated air, was often seen at concours d'élégance. This example has donned a sort of
automotive party frock, thanks to special equipment supplied by Renault's SAPRAR subsidiary.
The extras include an extended grille, twin spotlamps, a special bumper and chrome rimbellishers.
(© PHOTOTHÈQUE RENAULT COMMUNICATION/DR)

Ford's prestige Lincoln Division changed character completely with the launch of its 1949 range. It was out with the old V12 and in with a new 5.5-litre sidevalve V8 shared with the F-7/F-8 truck range. A brand new and reassuringly curvaceous body designed by E.T. Gregorie featured 'sunken' headlamps recessed into the wings. This Lincoln Cosmopolitan type 9 EH Sport Sedan is on trade plates. Note the rear-hinged 'suicide' back doors. (© GILLES BLANCHET COLLECTION)

Opposite below: Nash simultaneously surprised its main competitors and its faithful clients with the monocoque 'Airflyte' range launched in October 1948. Its basic shape, designed by Bob Koto, was one of the few production models of its day to be wind tunnel tested and showed a drag of just 113 lb at 60 mph. This Ambassador Series 60 shown at the Vichy concours d'élégance is fitted with optional spotlamps on the bumper and a moveable searchlight on the screen pillar.

(© MUSÉE DE L'OPÉRA DE VICHY)

Above: A wonderful make-believe hunting scene at the concours organised by the spa town of Vichy in the summer of 1949. The car is a 1949 model Chevrolet Styleline DeLuxe shooting brake whose upper body was framed in real wood; later models that year had an all-steel body with imitation wood appliqués. The model was rare in its day, with an output of just 3342 units that year; it's even rarer nowadays.

(© MUSÉE DE L'OPÉRA DE VICHY)

All the ingredients for a top-rank concours are here on the banks of the Lac d'Enghien, including sunny weather, on a June afternoon in 1950, a pretty girl dressed in style, a little dog as white as his mistress's dress, and of course a car neatly kitted out with accessories to suit the occasion. Hail the brand new Renault 4 CV Découvrable soft-top saloon! (© PHOTOTHÈQUE RENAULT COMMUNICATION/DR)

An irresistible combination: this 1950 Talbot-Lago Grand Sport T26 GS with Franay cabriolet coachwork is accompanied by a charming young lady dressed in the 'New Look' style launched by Christian Dior in 1947 that re-established Paris as the centre of the world of fashion. (© GILLES BLANCHET COLLECTION)

Above: French-born American industrial designer Raymond Loewy opened a styling studio inside the Studebaker plant at South Bend, Indiana, in 1939. From 1949–55 this restricted-access facility was headed by the talented Robert E. Bourke, who created the 'bullet nose' seen on this concept car based on the 1947 Studebaker Champion. The front-end treatment was reprised in modified form on the 1950–51 Studebakers and borrowed by Ford for its 1949 range, thanks to some unofficial moonlighting by Bourke.

(© GILLES BLANCHET COLLECTION)

Opposite, above: This beflagged Renault 4 CV with the pretty chauffeuse seen at the 1950 Enghien concours is named 'La Luciole' (Firefly). The accessory brightwork seems a little over the top for such a humble car. EPAF stainless steel wheel discs and whitewall tyres certainly weren't standard, nor were the twin horns, radio aerials and extra chrome beadings.

(© PHOTOTHÈQUE RENAULT COMMUNICATION/DR)

With a rather clumsy nose job by Carrosserie Esclassan of Boulogne, this 1949 Renault 4 CV rejoices in the name of 'Splendiluxe'. Apart from the overlong muzzle, the rest of the car is unchanged. The fanciful wheel trims are very much in the spirit of the age.
(© PHOTOTHÈQUE RENAULT COMMUNICATION/DR)

Britain's motor manufacturers were being exhorted to 'export or die', and the Austin A90 Atlantic launched at the 1948 London Show had been styled with the lucrative American market in mind. Handled in France by a Neuilly agency, 'this elegant convertible cabriolet' – here seen by the Lac d'Enghien – had electrically-operated top and windows. Sadly for Austin, sales were disappointing, even though the Atlantic of Madame de Vries and her poodle Ubu won the ACF Cup at the Bois de Boulogne concours in June 1949. (© GILLES BLANCHET COLLECTION)

Based in Paris, Émile Darl'Mat had become Peugeot's most important concessionaire in France and in the 1930s was renowned for his Peugeot conversions, notably the 301, 601 and 402 Éclipse retractable hardtops and the Darl'Mat Spécial Sport roadsters and coupés. From 1949, Darl'Mat again took up the conversion of Peugeots and this new 203 with special bonnet trim has been lowered by 5.5 inches and fitted with a special inlet manifold with twin carburettors to give a top speed of 80 mph.

(© GILLES BLANCHET COLLECTION)

This bird's eye view of the interior of
the Renault 4 CV Découvrable shown
reveals that while the somewhat basic
dashboard of the car is unchanged,
it has been 'accessoried' with a
Quillery 'anti-vibration' multi-spoke
steering wheel and a radio mounted
in the glove pocket.

The very first production examples of the Porsche 356, built in 1950-51, are certainly the purest, with a fine simplicity, maybe a bit rough round the edges but retaining the clean lines of the original prototypes from Gmünd. The air-cooled VW flat-four engine developed just 40 or 44 hp dependent on engine size (1100cc or 1300cc) but 85 mph was attainable thanks to the slippery shape.

(© GILLES BLANCHET COLLECTION)

Both native-born Italians, Simca founder Théodore Pigozzi and carrossier Joseph Figoni were on excellent terms, which from 1949 resulted in smart cabriolets and special coupés based on Simca 8 and Simca Sport chassis. An example is this smart drophead with a definite Italian air posing on the judging ramps at the 1950 concours d'élégance in the Place Vendôme in central Paris.

(© GILLES BLANCHET COLLECTION)

For the 1952 season the nationalised Régie Renault launched an attack on the middle-class saloon market with the new Frégate, though history reveals that it failed to live up to the high expectations placed on it. However, at the time it was important to demonstrate the worth of this comfortable 11 CV saloon to potential customers, as seen here at the Vichy concours d'élégance, where a fleet of four Frégates sailed by the attentive spectators. (© E-T-A-I ARCHIVES)

Henri Chapron was a favourite coachbuilder of Delahaye;
matching elegance to the marque's proud tradition, he
added a skilfully-measured touch of audacity. This example
is a Type 135 Dandy cabriolet that may have been
stylistically a little old hat, yet it still ably held its own at
the concours organised at the Bagatelle Polo Club in 1950.

Concours d'élégance were appreciated for their contribution to the local economy. Held under the patronage of a senior official of the Automobile Club de l'Ouest and organised by the Syndicat d'Initiative of Touraine, the concours d'élégance which took place in the Jardin des Prébendes in Tours on Sunday 10 September 1950 was split into two categories: Class A, open to concessionaires, encompassed French and foreign cars, open or closed and was subdivided into 5-10 CV, 10-16 CV and over 16 CV categories; Class B was identical, but restricted to private owners. (© GILLES BLANCHET COLLECTION)

In March 1953, the coachbuilders Bernard Pichon & André Parat of Sens (Yonne) unveiled this neat fastback coupé on a Panhard Dyna Junior, seen here at the concours held on the banks of the Lac d'Enghien. While attracting a sporting clientele, this stylish car also offered far greater comfort than the works-built cabriolet. The 'portholes' in the front wings are a styling cue first seen on 1949 Buicks. (© GILLES BLANCHET COLLECTION)

Above: When it was announced in the winter of 1948, the Ford Vedette was the only French-made production car to benefit from the flexibility and silent running of a V8 power unit, in this case a sidevalve 2.2-litre engine first seen on the Strasbourg-built Matford range of the mid-1930s. Originally conceived as a small car for the American market, it had been snapped up by Ford-France boss Maurice Dollfus when the USA programme was stillborn. This cabriolet on dealer plates is replete with extras: spotlights, whitewalls, radio and full hubcaps.

(© GILLES BLANCHET COLLECTION)

Right: A competitor's eye view of the judges' stand at the restaurant of the Grande Cascade in the Bois de Boulogne on 26 June 1951, with the two presenters standing in front, ready to greet each entry with flattering descriptions of the cars and their occupants. One wonders what they said at the June 1949 Grande Cascade concours when superstar Josephine Baker drove up on an MAP agricultural tractor! (© GILLES BLANCHET COLLECTION)

Quite unrecognisable as a Renault 4 CV apart from the distinctive wheel centres as the rear air intake, this smart roadster shown at the Lac d'Enghien in 1950 is the creation of the coachbuilder Duriez of Paris, founded in 1946. The overhang of the chunky front end gives the little car a rather ponderous profile. (© GILLES BLANCHET COLLECTION)

The creation of the Kaiser-Frazer group in 1947 by industry veteran Joseph Frazer and shipbuilding tycoon Henry J. Kaiser sent shockwaves through America's automobile industry. This 1953 Kaiser Manhattan posed on the shores of the Lac d'Enghien was undoubtedly the most aesthetically up-to-date of all the offerings from the world's mass-producers, and many makers would copy its styling features in years to come. Sadly, its sidevalve straight six was not as modern as the styling. (© GILLES BLANCHET COLLECTION)

Above: Biarritz, summer 1952, and this happy family group is posing in front of the impressive front end of a Renault Frégate registered in the Seine département that March. The spotlight came as standard. Sadly, the early Frégates were marred by a noisy, gutless engine, parasitic vibrations in the bodywork and fragile synchromesh in the gearbox. (© GILLES BLANCHET COLLECTION)

As sturdily British as roast beef, this appealing Austin A40 Somerset drophead photographed in front of the Casino at the Lac d'Enghien was a sub-contract conversion by Carbodies. The three-position top is typical of convertible bodies by this Coventry firm, using the folding B-pillar as a handy attachment for the rolled hood material in the town car position. (© GILLES BLANCHET COLLECTION)

Stultified by the personal preferences of chairman Kaufmann T. Keller, the ponderous styling of the '53 Chryslers had a detrimental effect on sales, and it was not until the '55 models designed by Virgil Exner appeared that things began to turn around. On the other hand, the big 'V' motif on the bonnet indicated the presence of one of the most up-to-date engines of the day, a hemi-head 5430cc V8 with overhead valves developing 180 hp at 4000 rpm. (© GILLES BLANCHET COLLECTION)

Above: Charmingly displayed
at a 1954 concours in
Bordeaux, the Autobleu coupé
was incontestably the most
successful special body on the
Renault 4 CV platform. It was
styled in Turin by Carrozzeria
Ghia, who carried out many
design exercises for Renault in
the 1950s, but Ghia had
insufficient production
facilities, so the Autobleu was
variously bodied by Figoni,
Pourtout and Chapron.
(© PHOTOTHÈQUE RENAULT
COMMUNICATION/DR)

Opposite, above: On Sunday 19 June 1954 the actor Jacques
Castelot (1914–1989), best-known for playing stuffy aristocrats,
took part in the *Journées Automobiles d'Enghien* at the wheel of a
13 CV Ford Comète coupé, accessorised with an eggcrate grille
similar to, but with a closer mesh, than that of the 22 CV Comète
Monte-Carlo. (© GILLES BLANCHET COLLECTION)

The work of the coachbuilder Mignot & Billebault of 125 Rue d'Aguesseau in Boulogne-Billancourt, this two-window, five/six seater drophead on the Ford Vedette chassis is distinguished by its full-length pontoon wing line, eliminating the slight swelling over the rear wheels of the production body. But such attention to detail came at a price: 740,000 francs for the basic car, plus another 90,000 francs for an electrically-operated top.

(© GILLES BLANCHET COLLECTION)

At the 1956 Paris salon, Henry Chapron unveiled a brand new design in coupé and cabriolet configuration baptised Mouette (seagull), built on the platform of the recently-introduced Renault Dauphine, which had been styled by Ghia. Though the bumpers framing the number plate were typical of the Billancourt product, the lines were stretched out, the seats were improved and, to save weight, the bonnet, boot and doors of the Chapron model were made of aluminium.

(© GILLES BLANCHET COLLECTION)

Despite the ready availability of the extremely attractive Simca Sport ex-works, the independent coachbuilder Figoni decided to construct special models on the Aronde platform. Typical is this cabriolet derived from the Florida saloon shown at the 1953 Paris Salon. The gloomy codfish appearance of the grille is a debatable feature. (© GILLES BLANCHET COLLECTION)

First seen at the October 1950 Paris Salon, the Reyonnah was a bizarre tandem-seated cyclecar invented by one M Hannoyer, who ran a repair shop near the Porte de Champerret in Paris. The front wheels were mounted at the end of parallelogram arms, which could be folded inwards to reduce the track, enabling the little car to be parked in the hallway of the owner's house or similar narrow access. Presented here by the doyenne of French actresses, the sparkling Pauline Dubost – born in 1910 and still going strong 100 years later – the Reyonnah was powered by a 175cc Ydral engine, but never found the mass market that its inventor anticipated. (© GILLES BLANCHET COLLECTION))

Built on the platform of the VW Beetle, the Volkswagen Karmann-Ghia coupé was the profitable fruit of the collaboration between the entrepreneurial Luigi Segre of Carrozzeria Ghia in Turin and coachbuilder Wilhelm Karmann of Osnabrück in Germany. Basically a scaled-down version of Virgil Exner's Ghia-Chrysler D'Excellence concept car, the Karmann-Ghia proved a great success, produced at the rate of up to 42,000 units a year from 1955. (© GILLES BLANCHET COLLECTION)

On a balmy Vietnamese night, this smartly-dressed couple are entering into the spirit of the Saigon concours d'élégance organised in February 1953, seemingly oblivious of the country's long-running civil war that would culminate in the battle of Diên Biên Phu. Their Renault 4 CV is equipped for the occasion with optional chromed wheels and whitewall tyres.
(© PHOTOTHÈQUE RENAULT COMMUNICATION/DR)

The masterstroke by the Studebaker Corporation in the postwar period was the launch of the 1953 range, styled by Raymond Loewy with considerable input from Bob Bourke. It debuted as the Starlight pillared coupé and the Starliner pillarless hardtop, and its sensationally low lines and long (120 in) wheelbase were tastefully restrained. In an era of fins and chrome, it failed to chime with American consumers. Seen at the Lac d'Enghien is this 1954 Starlight V8. (© GILLES BLANCHET COLLECTION)

In 1954 Oldsmobile ranked fourth among American manufacturers, with sales of 433, 810 units that year. French motorists with a taste for American styling – and with the funds to indulge it – could have ordered this rare Super 88 cabriolet (6452 built) from the Parisian General Motors concessionaire SADVA. It had an ohv V8 developing 185 hp. (© GILLES BLANCHET COLLECTION)

Above: At the Concours d'élégance in Tournai, Belgium, in June 1955, this Renault Frégate Amiral proudly displays the model's new oval grille with its central transverse bar, a design largely inspired by the Ghia Ondine prototype shown at the Paris Salon of October 1953. This two-tone saloon has an external 'eyebrow' sun visor and a number of the accessory embellishments that were fashionable in the '50s.

(© PHOTOTHÈQUE RENAULT COMMUNICATION/ MAISON DE LA PHOTO)

Opposite below: Back on the Grand-Place in Tournai in Belgium during the summer of 1955, this heavily accessorised Renault 4 CV seems dwarfed by the young lady in the floral dress posing in front of the jury – or is it just a photographic illusion? Happily, she's not as heavily made up as the little car with its multitudinous chrome embellishments. (© PHOTOTHÈQUE RENAULT COMMUNICATION/MAISON DE LA PHOTO)

Above: The skilled Philippe Charbonneaux penned the lines of the plastic-bodied barchetta on a Salmson 2300 Sport chassis in 1954. The charming lady is Marie-Claire Cibié, an engineer and one of the announcers at the Le Mans 24 Hour race.

(© GILLES BLANCHET COLLECTION)

Three main French coachbuilders – Chapron, Mignot & Billebault and Letourneur & Marchand – were interested in transforming the middle-market Renault Frégate into elegant coupés and – in particular – cabriolets. This is Letourneur & Marchand's interpretation posing before the jury at the Lac d'Enghien concours, sponsored by the monthly magazine *L'Action Automobile*, in June 1955.
(© PHOTOTHÈQUE RENAULT COMMUNICATION/DR)

Franay didn't believe in unnecessary wastefulness: this cabriolet built on a Talbot Lago T26 GS Grand Sport chassis in the winter of 1953 is a reconstruction created after the first chassis – first shown at the 1949 Paris Salon – was involved in an accident. With an egg-crate grille reminiscent of the Ferrari 212, this handsome machine has a well-balanced appearance.
(© GILLES BLANCHET COLLECTION)

The rear view of the Letourneur & Marchand Frégate cabriolet reveals the feature that distinguishes it from its competitors: the little round tail lights set at the tip of the vestigial tailfins. Praiseworthy is the neat downcurving side strake delineating the essential two-tone colour scheme. Again, style came at a price, for the Letourneur & Marchand Frégate cost a hefty 1,300,000 francs, against 395,000 francs for the austere, but nonetheless functional, 4 CV Affaires.

(© PHOTOTHÈQUE RENAULT COMMUNICATION/DR)

Designed in Dearborn, Michigan, by Ford, the Versailles V8 was born again as a Simca after the French company took over the Ford-France factory at Poissy in autumn 1954 when the American giant sold off the unprofitable manufacturing side of its French subsidiary. Bearing all the stylistic hallmarks of its American parentage, this Versailles appears to have the optional Vistadome sunshine roof.

(© GILLES BLANCHET COLLECTION)

The 948cc Austin Healey Sprite announced on 20 May 1958 was a bargain-basement sports car using off-the-shelf parts from the Austin A35 family saloon, conceived at the behest of BMC chairman Sir Leonard Lord to complement the successful Austin-Healey 100. The protruding 'frog-eye' lamps were a cash-saving alternative to the original concept of retractable headlights. In France it cost a hefty 1,195,000 francs, 3000 francs more than an Alpine A-106 cabriolet.

(© GILLES BLANCHET COLLECTION)

An odd choice of names was applied to the 1957 Simca Sport range, for this handsome cabriolet was christened 'Océane' while the coupé was named 'Plein-Ciel' (open sky). Nevertheless, the two models were extremely attractive, not least for their build quality by Facel (Forges & Ateliers de Construction d'Eure-et-Loir), founded in 1939 by Jean Daninos. This drophead cost a cool 1,064,000 francs. (© GILLES BLANCHET COLLECTION)

Originally conceived as a new, limited production, Healey model, the shapely Austin-Healey 100/4 was adopted as a mainstream BMC model after the corporation's chairman Sir Leonard Lord saw the prototype at the 1952 London Motor Show and made Donald Healey an offer he couldn't refuse. The fold-flat windscreen and knock-off wire wheels underlined its sporting credentials. Over 14,000 'Healey Hundreds' were built from 1953-56. (© GILLES BLANCHET COLLECTION)

Most French motorists in 1956 could only dream of driving a Cadillac Eldorado Biarritz convertible, for this 5986cc V8 extravaganza was a car strictly for the very wealthy. It was also a rarity on European roads, for the Cadillac factory in Detroit only turned out 2,150 examples of the Eldorado Biarritz convertible that model year. This fashionable ensemble at the Lac d'Enghien at least enabled the envious spectators to fantasise about owning one! (© GILLES BLANCHET COLLECTION)

In contrast to its rivals from Cadillac, Packard and Chrysler (Imperial), the
Lincoln Capri Premiere hardtop coupé – seen here in front of the Enghien Casino
on 23 June 1956 – pointed the way to the styling future, for it was relatively
unadorned with chrome gewgaws. The 'eyebrows' over the headlamps were
a feature first seen on the 1955 Lincoln Futura double-bubble cockpit
'dream car', which had a bizarre afterlife when it was converted into the
original TV 'Batmobile'. (© GILLES BLANCHET COLLECTION)

Above: This Silver Dawn cabriolet seen at the Lac d'Enghien concours in 1956 is one of the rare open bodies built on this chassis. Since no open models were listed by the factory, convertible Dawns were bodied to special order; this elegant long-wing drophead is bodied by Chapron, chassis number LSTH79. It would have been sold by Franco-Britannic Automobiles of Paris, the Rolls-Royce distributor for France.

(© GILLES BLANCHET COLLECTION)

Right: Sold in France through the Weisman company of 64 de Avenue Victor Hugo in Paris, the Ford Thunderbird was already into its second year of production when this photograph was taken. A Thunderbird was the favourite car of James Bond author Ian Fleming rather than a Bentley or an Aston Martin, but here the T-Bird is presented by a lovely model named Fortunia.

(© GILLES BLANCHET COLLECTION)

The Mercedes-Benz 300SL gullwing coupé, the first sports car developed by Daimler-Benz after the war, was produced at the behest of USA importer Max Hoffman. The 300SL programme began in September 1953 and the 300SL was launched at the New York Sports Car Show the following February. Its spaceframe, weighing just 110 lb, had high sills, making conventional doors impossible, hence the top-hinged 'gullwings'. The 3-litre straight-six engine had fuel injection – a production first – enabling a top speed of 160 mph. In France it cost a staggering 6,385,000 francs. (© GILLES BLANCHET COLLECTION)

The Mercury, the Ford Motor Company's marque – costlier than a Ford, cheaper than a Lincoln – dated from 1939. This six-seater Montclair convertible, top of the 1956 Mercury range, was rarely seen on French roads, for overall production in the Mercury plant in Detroit was only 7762 units, most of which were sold on the home market. (© GILLES BLANCHET COLLECTION)

Over-large, over-heavy, over-decorated and over here, the vast Imperial Crown convertible was powered by a 6445cc V8 developing 325 hp and weighed a massive 2.4 tons. Imperial had become a separate marque in 1955, but lacked the prestige of the rival Cadillac badge. The 1957 season was the marque's best, the only one in which it out-sold Lincoln. That year, 1167 convertibles were sold; thereafter soft-top sales languished around the 500-700 mark. (© GILLES BLANCHET COLLECTION)

No serious French concours would have been complete in 1957 without the presence of an Alpine A106/1062. This iconic sports marque was built in Dieppe from 1955 by Renault dealer Jean Rédélé, with laminated polyester bodywork on a Renault 4 CV platform. Its 747cc engine was available in various tuning states from 21 hp to 42 hp for the hotshot Alpine A106/1063 'Mille Miles' version. (© GILLES BLANCHET COLLECTION)

Built on a Panhard Dyna Junior platform, this swoopy roadster was created in the shops of Vivez in Bordeaux, a company that carried out subcontract work for Pichon & Parat. A whole industry grew up among small coachbuilders and bodyshops in creating sports bodywork on the humble platforms of the utilitarian air-cooled flat-twin Panhard Dyna and the rear-engined Renault 4 CV. (© GILLES BLANCHET COLLECTION)

Above: Even concept cars were welcome at the Lac d'Enghien concours, in this case the Packard Pan American sports car, first seen at the 1952 New York International Motor Sports Show. It was bodied by John W. Henney & Son of Freeport, Illinois, a company founded in 1885 to manufacture wagons and in more recent times best-known for hearses and formal limousines. The Pan American was exhibited at a number of European motor shows, hence its presence in Enghien.

(© GILLES BLANCHET COLLECTION)

Opposite, above: Drophead versions of the big Austin A 125 Sheerline – normally seen with heavy limousine bodywork – were extremely rare. Pennock of The Hague built one for Queen Juliana of the Netherlands in 1952, and this high-waisted two-door coupé seen at the Lac d'Enghien is obviously a one-off by an enterprising coachbuilder.

(© GILLES BLANCHET COLLECTION)

With its thrusting 'Dagmar' front bumper, wraparound windscreen with 'dogleg' pillars and elaborate chrome wheel discs, this Cadillac Eldorado Seville hardtop coupé on New York plates is one of just 2100 examples built in the 1957 model year. On 15 June that year this hymn to opulence, with a thirsty 6-litre V8 developing 325 hp at 4800 rpm beneath its massive bonnet, strutted its stuff in front of the Enghien Casino.

(© GILLES BLANCHET COLLECTION)

In 1956 the handsome Simca 'Sport Week-End' drophead and the closed 'Coupé de Ville' adopted, in common with the mainstream models of the Poissy marque, the 1300cc 'Flash-Spécial' power unit, which developed 57 hp against the old engine's 45 hp. This two-tone 'Coupé de Ville' is being shown in front of an appreciative audience at Enghien. (© GILLES BLANCHET COLLECTION)

In 1955 engineer Jean-Albert Grégoire created this elegant front-wheel drive drophead, whose considerable front overhang is due to the forward-mounted air-cooled flat-four power unit. The first French road car with disc brakes, it was bodied by Henri Chapron in consultation with Grégoire, who claimed the design was later poached by Lancia for the Flaminia Sport. Few were sold, and Grégoire stated he lost 1.5 million francs on each one. (© GILLES BLANCHET COLLECTION)

Société Anonyme d'Exploitation
DES
GARAGES MORIN Frères
Au Capital de 806.000 fr.

Concessionnaire "CITROËN"

Directeur : H. MANDUCHET

Boulevard Loche-et-Matras

LOUDUN (Vienne)

Téléphone 42

R. C. LOUDUN 2930 B
C. CHÈQUES POSTAUX
LIMOGES 624-47

Loudun, le 14 AVRIL 1956

Etablissements P I C H A R D
Concessionnaire CITROEN
Avenue Grammont

T O U R S

V/Réf. ....

N/Réf. ....

Monsieur et Cher Collègue,

Le COMITE DES FETES DE LA VILLE DE LOUDUN, qui organise, le DIMANCHE
I3 MAI I956, un GRAND CONCOURS d'ELEGANCE AUTOMOBILES ET SCOOTERS, vous demande
d'y faire participer votre Clientèle et Vous-même si vous le désirez.

Je vous demande d'être l'interprête auprès de l'Ecurie et MOTO-CLUB
de votre Ville pour les inciter à participer à cette Manifestation.

Vous trouverez ci-joint des imprimés concernant le Réglement et des
Fiches d'Engagement.

De très beaux PRIX EN ESPECES sont offerts aux SCOOTERS et VOITURES
Classés, ainsi que plusieurs COUPES, dont tout particulièrement celle offerte
par la VILLE DE LOUDUN.

En vous remerciant à l'avance, je m'excuse de vous mettre à contribution et vous prie d'accepter l'expression de mes sentiments les meilleurs.

H. MANDUCHET

P. S.- Si vous êtes livré d'une D.S. I9, peut-être
pourriez-vous y faire participer votre Client
ou Vous-même, ce qui réhausserait l'éclat de
cette Manifestation et dont le DOUBLE CHEVRON
ne pourrait que s'en enorgueillir.
Je compte donc sur votre présence.

Pièces détachées "CITROEN" garanties d'origine

In April 1956 Citroën concessionaire Henri Manduchet of Loudun (Vienne) invited his friendly rival Pichard of Tours to be the presenter at the 'Grand Concours d'Élégance des Automobiles et Scooters' in Loudun the next month. The revolutionary – controversial, even – Citröen DS had been launched at the 1955 Paris Salon, but was obviously in short supply, for as a 'by the way' PS, Manduchet added: 'If you've taken delivery of a DS19, could your client – or even yourself – take part with it, as it will add glamour to the occasion.'

(© GILLES BLANCHET COLLECTION)

The future looked bright for Borgward of Bremen when this Borgward 1500 saloon posed at the 9th Journée Automobile d'Enghien in 1956. Carl Borgward had bounced back after his factories were badly damaged in the war, bringing out Germany's first all-new postwar car in 1949. But sales were never quite high enough, and by 1960 the company was in deep financial trouble. Ford rejected the chance to buy Borgward and production ended in 1961. (© GILLES BLANCHET COLLECTION)

Concours d'Élégance Automobile du 13 Mai 1956

organisé par le **Comité des Fêtes de la Ville de LOUDUN**

sous la Haute Autorité de l'**Automobile-Club de l'Ouest**

FICHE D'ENGAGEMENT

Nom du Concurrent : _____

Prénoms : _____

Lieu d'Habitation : _____

Département : _____

Ci-joint la somme de { **300 fr.** pour l'Engagement d'un **SCOOTER** (1)
{ **1.000 fr.** « « d'une **VOITURE** (1)

Somme à verser à la convenance du Concurrent, ou par CHÈQUE POSTAL, ou BANCAIRE, au nom de :
Monsieur Georges BOUDINEAU, Secrétaire du Comité des Fêtes, Rue Carnot, LOUDUN (Vienne)

(1) Rayer la mention inutile

IMP. FIRMIN-BLANCHARD - LOUDUN

This was the entry form for cars and scooters at the Loudun concours d'élégance, held under the patronage of the enterprising Automobile Club de l'Ouest, organisers of the Le Mans 24-hour race. Intriguingly, while it asks for the would-be contestant's name and address, it fails to ask what make or model of car or scooter he proposes to display!

(© GILLES BLANCHET COLLECTION)

In 1955 Talbot of Suresnes unveiled its T14 LS (Lago Sport) coupé, initially powered by an anaemic four-cylinder engine, and later by the much more vigorous BMW V8 from the 502, giving a claimed top speed of 125 mph. In this form, and with an air scoop over the bonnet, the car was hopefully named 'America', but the anticipated sales just weren't there. Production was a miserable thirteen. Displaying the America model at Enghien on 14 June 1958 are Yves Giraud-Cabantous, builder from 1936–38 of Caban cyclecars and sports cars, and the Czech actress Eva Linkova.

(© GILLES BLANCHET COLLECTION)

The Torinese master coachbuilder Alfredo Vignale created the body for this 1957 Ferrari type 212 Inter seen at Enghien. The falling roofline was a classic trick by coachbuilders of sporting coupés to give an impression of speed. The chromed strakes on the front wings are less successful. Vignale's golden days with Ferrari were the years 1950-53, when he built over 100 bodies for the Maranello marque; after that, he was elbowed out by Pininfarina. He later bodied 242 Maserati 3500GT cabriolets. (© GILLES BLANCHET COLLECTION)

Surprisingly, the well-proportioned bodywork of this Grand Touring coupé sits on the humble platform of a middle-class Renault Frégate. Less surprisingly, this is an entirely Italian project, the result of a collaboration between former Ghia boss Mario Boano, who designed the body, and tuning wizard Carlo Abarth, who spiced up the humdrum powerplant from Billancourt with a new induction system using twin Weber carburettors. Production by Autobleu was considered, but cost considerations ruled this out. (© GILLES BLANCHET COLLECTION)

Even more frog-eyed than the Austin-Healey Sprite, the rare Panhard Dyna type Z-17 cabriolet had two distinctive features on the French market: it was a comfortable full four-seater and it had two rear side glasses that acted as useful wind deflectors when the top was down. The bodyside beading framing the two-tone paint job is also noteworthy. From spring 1956 this model was powered by the air-cooled flat-twin 'Tigre' engine developing 50 hp. (© GILLES BLANCHET COLLECTION)

With the Château de Vincennes as a backdrop, this couple seem well pleased with their Peugeot 403 cabriolet on a fine day in July 1958 that enables them to take full advantage of the droptop configuration. This model was launched in 1957 at the price of 1,250,000 francs, which seemed rather prohibitive in spite of the high quality of manufacture.

(© GILLES BLANCHET COLLECTION)

Opposite below: The evergreen actor Fernand Luguet (1892–1979) is leaning against the recently-launched Facel Vega Excellence four-door limousine, a model first shown at the 1956 Paris Salon but not homologated with the Service des Mines until Spring 1958. The Excellence was powered by Facel's engine of choice, a big Chrysler V8, in this case a 6.5-litre unit. A three-speed TorqueFlight automatic transmission was standard, with a four-speed Pont-à-Mousson manual 'box optional. Just 152 Excellences were built before production ended in 1960. (© GILLES BLANCHET COLLECTION)

Above: Once again, USA foreign car dealer Max Hoffman was the catalyst for an iconic sports car. At his urging, BMW hired industrial designer Count Albrecht Goertz, who penned two sporty models, the 503 coupé and the 507 roadster, which had its world premiere in New York's Waldorf-Astoria hotel in 1955. Powered by a 3.2-litre V8 engine, the elegant 507 was good for 120 mph. Production was limited, totalling just 253 units between 1956–59. (© GILLES BLANCHET COLLECTION)

The curious little Nash Metropolitan sub-compact launched in the spring of 1954 had been conceived in the studios of the Nash-Kelvinator Corporation of America but was built in England by Austin and used their 1200cc ohv A40 engine allied to a three-speed transmission and A30 back axle. It was originally intended for American markets only, and in late 1954 it was announced that the Metropolitan would also be available through Hudson dealerships. This is the 1956-57 Hudson version at the Lac d'Enghien. (© GILLES BLANCHET COLLECTION)

With the evocative name of Chambord, the new top-of-the-range model of the Vedette division of Simca went on sale in 1958. It continued the concept of a luxurious and comfortable saloon agreeably styled in keeping with current fashion. Its smooth 2.3-litre sidevalve V8 power unit had come with the purchase of Ford-France's Poissy plant in 1954; its basic design dated back to 1935. Demand for the Simca Vedette line-up, which consisted of the Beaulieu, Chambord, Marly and Présidence ranges, was relatively limited: in 1959 production of all the Vedettes was just 15,966 compared with 194,553 examples of the popular Aronde and P-60 models.

(© GILLES BLANCHET COLLECTION)

The 1959 season saw America's top producer Chevrolet lose its crown to Ford, which built 1,528,592 units against Chevy's 1,428,962. But French Chevrolet fans could console themselves by ordering an Impala convertible like this from the French concessionaire Duvivier. Beneath a bonnet like the flight deck of an aircraft carrier beat a 5.7-litre ohv V8 developing a lazy 315 hp.

The dynamism of Studebaker's French importer Dujardin did much to further the distribution of the American marque in France. This 1956 Golden Hawk five-seat hardtop coupé was the South Bend factory's top of the range sporty model, though production that model year was just 4071 units. Power – 275 hp at 4600 rpm – came from a 5.8-litre five-bearing ohv V8 originally designed by Packard, which had merged with Studebaker on 22 June 1954, only to go out of production four years later. (© GILLES BLANCHET COLLECTION)

The suave fellow in the sharp double-breasted suit seems more intent on kissing the hand of the lady in the frou-frou skirt than admiring the aesthetic success that is the Arista 'de Passy', a limited production plastic-bodied coupé produced under the aegis of Parisian Panhard concessionaire Raymond Gaillard and built on the platform of the 5 CV Dyna. Sadly, the production costs inescapable with hand-built cars dictated a purchase price of 1,580,000 francs, seriously hindering sales. (© GILLES BLANCHET COLLECTION)

Sir William Lyons of Jaguar, like Jean Daninos in France, was very much in control of styling at his company. While the Mk IX Jaguar launched in 1958 was little changed in appearance from the previous Mk VIII, it had represented a considerable technical advance with the adoption of all-round disc brakes. Power was increased, too, with a 3.8-litre XK engine rather than the old model's 3.4-litre unit. (© GILLES BLANCHET COLLECTION)

Aston Martin was justly proud of the DB4 launched in 1958 which it summarised as 'the sports car of the century'. Its sleek coupé body had been penned by Federico Formenti of Carrozzeria Touring of Milan, which also contributed its 'Superleggera' construction, with alloy body panels fastened to a rigid skeleton frame of light steel tubes. Power was provided by an all-new 3.7-litre dohc straight-six developing 240 hp. (© GILLES BLANCHET COLLECTION)

Above: Were the lovely twins really impressed by the awkward lines of the 1957 Rambler sedan, a sort of rolling caricature of the excesses of transatlantic styling? It's doubtful. At least the driver is happy, because – to paraphrase architect Frank Lloyd Wright – by sitting in this product of the USA's fourth-biggest manufacturer, he doesn't have to look at it...

(© GILLES BLANCHET COLLECTION)

Right: In 1952 Alfa Romeo decided to offer 200 copies of a prototype sports coupé designed by Felice Mario Boano of Ghia as prizes for a lottery to raise funds for a new mass-produced model, but the little Ghia shop couldn't handle the order, which went to Bertone. The result was the Alfa Giulietta Sprint, and Bertone built some 40,000 examples between 1953-66, putting the Torinese coachbuilder into the big time as an industrialised coachbuilder and creating a modern classic.

(© GILLES BLANCHET COLLECTION)

It was a brave decision by coachbuilder Jean Daninos of Facel-Metallon to decide to enter the luxury market in 1954 with a car designed to regain France's lost dominance of this field. Daninos was the driving force in developing the car, responsible for the project engineering and basic styling, aided by chief engineer Jacques Brasseur. Production of his original FV3 model ran from 1954 until the summer of 1957, about the time that this photograph was taken at the Enghien concours. Power came from a compact modern ohv 4940cc Chrysler hemi-head V8, an excellent choice for such a car, giving sparkling acceleration and a top speed of over 125 mph, outstanding for 1954. (© GILLES BLANCHET COLLECTION)

On 4 September 1957 Ford launched a new marque, the Edsel, intended to fill a perceived gap in the middle-market. It was styled by Roy Brown, who had worked at Cadillac and LaSalle before joining Lincoln in 1953. The controversial 'horse-collar' radiator grille was apparently adopted to solve cooling problems with the Edsel's big V8 power units. Sales proved disappointing and the Edsel – this is the 1958 Pacer convertible, of which only 1876 were made – was killed off in 1960.

(© GILLES BLANCHET COLLECTION)

It's apparent that as the 1950s drew to a close, the glory days of the concours d'élégance were over. Custom bodies were almost extinct. Even the smart Drauz-bodied Porsche 356A Speedster, with its distinctive chrome side strake, was a production model; however only 556 found owners in the 1958 model year. Happily, concours d'élégance have seen a revival in recent years, with elegant classic cars vying for supremacy on the manicured lawns of such venues as Pebble Beach and Meadowbrook in the USA and Villa d'Este, Bagatelle and Goodwood in Europe. The glamour remains, but the girls have gone… (© GILLES BLANCHET COLLECTION)

Acknowledgments

The author is deeply grateful to the following people, without whom this book would never have seen the light of day. First among equals is the incomparable Gilles Blanchet with his marvellous photographic record of the great days of the concours d'élégance, not forgetting Josette Alviset of the Musée de l'Opéra de Vichy, the effervescent Claude Le Maître of the Société d'Histoire du Groupe Renault, Frédérique Berry of the Renault photographic archives and Anne-Marie Michel of the Photothèque Citroën.

Of course, this book is dedicated to my beloved Mimi, who, thanks to her natural poise, could have graced the most stunning prewar coachwork, nor must we forget that matchless couple, my son William and his wife, Nadia, whose little Louise will unquestionably be an elegant lady of renown in the future.

Naturally, this work is also dedicated to my friends Dominique Pascal – who in 1995 published (with ETAI) a book on this engrossing subject – and Jean-François Krause, who has been a faultless source of assistance on every occasion.

Index of coachbuilders

Design (French edition)	Carine Deligey
Jacket design (US edition)	Simon Loxley
Printer	Toppan Leefung Printers Ltd
Printing	Heidelberg-5C CD102-5-LX
Page size	240mm × 290mm
Text paper	157gsm Japan NPI gloss art
End papers	140gsm China Gold Sun woodfree
Dust jacket	157gsm Korea HI-Q gloss art
Inks	TOKA.INK
Body text	11/14pt Arno Pro
Captions	10/12pt Cambria